Santa Bar...

Volu...

December 2018

MW00880532

Editrix

Silver Webb

Editors

Laura Hemenway, Mistress of Song

Ron Alexander, the Poetry Baron

Guest Editor of Poetry

Sharon Venezio

Consigliere

Matthew Pallamary

Éminence Grise

Señor McTavish

Contributors

<table>
<tr><td>Cathryn Beeks</td><td>Ian McCartor</td></tr>
<tr><td>Donna Lynn Caskey</td><td>M.K. Knight</td></tr>
<tr><td>Lisa Cheby</td><td>Tom Layou</td></tr>
<tr><td>Ted Chiles</td><td>Gabrielle Louise</td></tr>
<tr><td>Nina Clements</td><td>Shelly Lowenkopf</td></tr>
<tr><td>Chella Courington</td><td>Jordan O'Halloran</td></tr>
<tr><td>Cyrus Cromwell</td><td>Nate Streeper</td></tr>
<tr><td>Gwen Dandridge</td><td>Max Talley</td></tr>
<tr><td>Nicholas Deitch</td><td>Justin Thompson</td></tr>
<tr><td>Kim Dower</td><td>Stephen T. Vessels</td></tr>
<tr><td>Yvonne M. Estrada</td><td>Robin Winter</td></tr>
<tr><td>Robin Gowen</td><td>Terry Wolverton</td></tr>
<tr><td>Annika Fehling</td><td>Chris Wozney</td></tr>
<tr><td>Yvette Keller</td><td></td></tr>
</table>

Santa Barbara Literary Journal
Santa Barbara, CA, U.S.A.
www.sblitjo.com

ISBN: 9781729127070

A special thanks to Robin Gowen for use of the cover art, "Shadow in the Vines."

Design of internal layout and cover by Angela Borda.

Santa Barbara Literary Journal

Volume 2: *Cor Serpentis*

Table of Contents

POEMS

6

DOWN THE RABBIT HOLE

ART

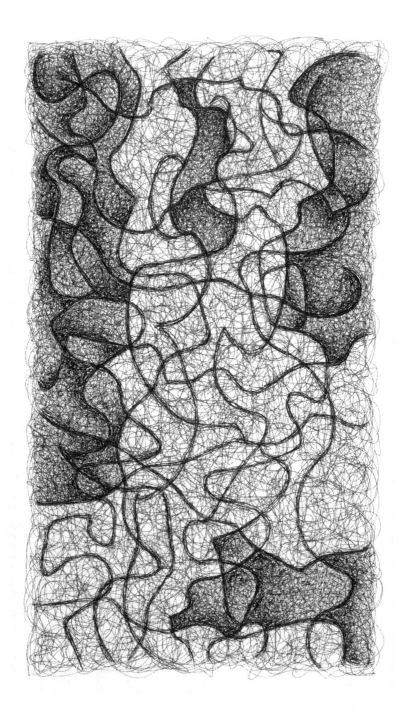

"Untitled October 1, 2015" by Stephen T. Vessels

LETTER FROM THE EDITRIX

by Silver Webb

Where do you go from Andromeda? Volume 1 of the *Santa Barbara Literary Journal*, titled "Andromeda," was only the beginning of what I hope will be a long run for this journal, which aims to show the best of Santa Barbara's writers, musicians, and artists. And our community extends further afield, to those who attend the Santa Barbara Writer's Conference or come into town regularly to play music, or simply those who are part of our nebulous trible of creative minds, spread all over the world. A family, if you will, of pens and guitar strings and paint brushes. These are the things my father taught me to value (along with a good coleslaw recipe and a pitcher of Budweiser).

To represent this interconnected family, I've decided to name each volume after a constellation. As Moby says, "We are all made of stars," and the constellation of the *Santa*

Barbara Literary Journal is nothing if not a family of bright lights, people who have chosen to make creative expression their priority. Without such communities, the world would be a dim place, indeed.

But what constellation for Volume 2? When I was doing what all good researchers do (i.e., looking at Wikipedia) and pondering the different names for constellations, one jumped out at me in particular. The *Serpens* Constellation, or the snake constellation. This snake, in star form, is held in the hands of Asclepius, the son of a Greek God, who learned how to heal by watching a snake regenerate. I could simply say that all writers and artists and musicians are snakelike, shedding their skin and constantly reinventing themselves, telling new stories, writing new songs. Well, the good ones do, anyway. But in that particular instant, I had snakes on my mind for another reason. And to discover what that is, you will need to read my interview of our featured author, Stephen T. Vessels, in the "Down the Rabbithole" section. I promise you that a snake will make an appearance there! Stephen's artwork also graces the pages of this volume, for which I thank him profusely.

Look carefully and you will see flickers of tongue and shiny scales all through the book. Medusa and her sisters appear in Poetry, something deadly lurks in Fiction. If you find yourself in church in one of our stories, you may just be hissed at. The cover art features a winsome snake ("Shadow in the Vines") that was painted specifically for this issue by the talented and prolific Robin Gowen, a woman who is just as generous with her paintbrushes as she is with her homemade bread and literary critique.

Some new additions have been made to our editorial team, all of whom are volunteers and have my heartfelt thanks. Aside from Our Mistress of Song, Laura Hemenway, and our Poetry Baron, Ron Alexander, we have Sharon Venezio as guest editor of poetry for this issue. In additon to our Consigliere Matt Pallamary, we have the Éminence Grise, both of whom give freely of their time for the cause of literature, if not the Editrix's equilibrium. I'd also like to thank Grace Rachow for her tireless cheerleading of all things literary in Santa Barbara.

I feel very lucky to be part of this community and honored to represent, to the best of my ability, the constellation of talent and heart inherent in it.

Best,
Silver Webb
The Editrix

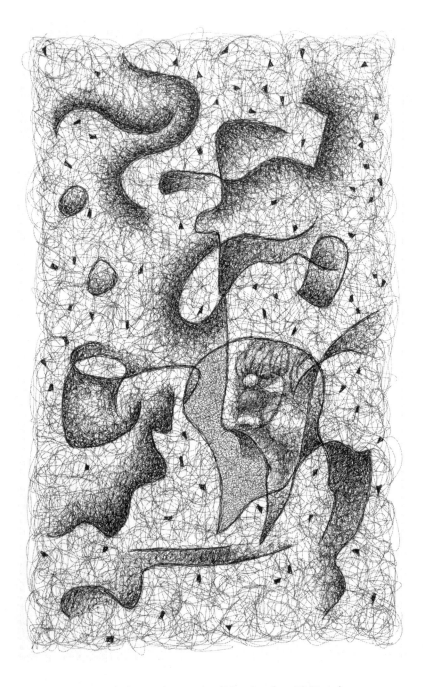

"Untitled March 18, 2016" by Stephen T. Vessels

FICTION

BLOW, WINDS, AND CRACK
YOUR CHEEKS

by Shelly Lowenkopf

"You missed a spot," Lucy told him. "Let me get that for you."

Matt Bender checked the mirror. No missed spot. When a stage manager tells you a spot's missing, yet every bump and crevice on your face covers to your satisfaction with Max Factor Lasting Performance Foundation, better watch out for lurking subtext. But no missed spot.

"At least let me do the wrinkles," Lucy said. "And you should know. Those guys? They're back. Again."

"Probably to see Stella." He pried the lid off the tin of black Shinola shoe polish to begin the wrinkles.

"Why are you being so stubborn? They called to make sure you were on. 'Is Matt Bender on as George tonight?' Their exact words. Besides, Stella doesn't get people from Hollywood. Stella gets non-equity theaters in Bakersfield. She gets county fairs, bowling alleys."

Bender suffered a wince on Stella's behalf. "Go," he said. "I need to finish my makeup."

"Hollywood," Lucy said. "Japanese denim jeans. Shiny Ermenegildo Zegna jackets. Here to see you."

"Go," Bender said.

"I could do the wrinkles for you."

Bender focused on being George for the performance. George, husband of Martha in *Who's Afraid of Virginia Woolf?* Far away in spirit as you could get from the original First Family, right? No difficulty overcoming curiosity about the two Hollywood guys in the audience. They could mean some TV work. Even so, men in Japanese denim jeans and Zegna jackets don't equate with offers to do *Lear*, do they? If someone wanted him to do *Lear*, that would be a different matter, wouldn't it?

He thrust the Hollywood guys out of his mind, squeezed George in place. You couldn't blame him for throwing a hint of Lear into his performance as George tonight. "Blow, winds, and crack your cheeks! Rage! Blow!" Couldn't blame him, could you?

At curtain call, they bowed to an appreciative audience. Stella gave Bender's hand a tug of admiration. "You rocked tonight," she said. "Energy all over the place."

Bender tugged back his thanks. Only then did he notice the empty seats the Hollywood guys once occupied. They could be in his dressing room, waiting for him. After two more curtain calls, he retreated backstage to find, instead, Digby, the director.

"Well, well," Digby said. He gave Bender a chiropractic hug. "Someone's found his voice, all right. Good on us, we've got another week in the run. Let's keep the performance at this level, shall we?"

Bender removed his makeup, dressed, expecting the Hollywood visitors to be waiting outside the stage door. But when he stepped into the night, he found Lucy. "Awesome work tonight," she said. "I've got a two-for-one coupon for Panda Express. Interested?"

"You barely touched your orange chicken."

"Sorry," Bender said. "I've had painful and unfortunate experiences with chicken."

Lucy reached across the table to take possession of his fork hand. "You certainly have an intriguing way of coming on to a girl." He felt the warmth of her hand, the intensity of her gaze. "How about," she said, "I take you home, fuck your brains out, you tell me about your poultry traumas?"

"I don't think that would be a good idea," Bender said.

Lucy reclaimed her hand. "Stella," she said. "Saving yourself for Stella."

"Nothing to do with Stella, and no, I'm not gay."

"Not like I'm looking for long-term commitment," Lucy said. "Run of the play. Farewell dinner on Sterns Wharf. Feed a few gulls with our leftovers. Then a goodbye hug at the dolphin fountain, and I go back to weeknight hostess at the

Chase Restaurant. You move on to—"

"Nothing yet," Bender said. "Vague prospects. Nevertheless, not a good idea."

"Okay," she said. "I get it. You're what, forty-six? And serious about what you do."

"Forty-eight."

Lucy reached for his plate. "Shame to let that orange chicken go to waste."

"You missed a spot," Stella told him. "Let me get that for you."

Bender checked the mirror. No missing spot, only subtext beyond his knowledge that Stella Ware was Mitzi Berliner's attempt at rebranding herself for theatrical impact.

Stella's subtext sent him a warning to be careful. "Thanks," he told her. "I think I've got it."

"Pretty cool," Stella said, "You with two dudes from Hollywood, front row, three times this week. Guess you don't have to worry about your next job."

Bender remembered what Lucy said about Stella's job prospects. "You shouldn't be here now," he said. "In less than ten minutes, I've got to own George's sarcasm and resentment toward your Martha."

"That's why I'm here," she said. "What a turn-on, the way you came at me last night. I could feel it. " She thumped her pelvis. "In here. It was," she smiled, "very sexual. So bring it on."

"Okay."

"And," she said.

"And?"

"Dinner. My place. Got a boatload of moo goo gai pan. Raoul, the sous chef at the Peking Palace, has a crush on me."

"Thanks," Bender said, "but I don't think that would be a good idea."

Stella nodded. "I get it," she said. "Lucy."

"Not Lucy," Bender said. "The essential ingredient of moo goo gai pan chicken."

Stella took this in for a moment. "Wow," she said. "Working with you is such a trip."

❖   ❖   ❖

"Surely you noticed them." Digby watched Bender towel off his makeup. "They've been front row center, three times. Tall, cadaverous sort and a more Falstaffian type."

"Zegna jackets, Japanese denim trousers."

"Good eye, my boy."

"I noticed," Bender said.

"They particularly wanted to know, were you happy here, doing *Who's Afraid?*"

"And you told them?"

"If he's half as happy as I am to have him in my cast, he'll be near delirious."

"Their response?"

"Each made notes on his iPad."

"How do you read all this?"

Digby spread his palms. "After this run, I have the

choice of directing *Alice in Wonderland* for Central High School in fucking Fresno, or unemployment insurance. You, on the other hand, appear to have a well-funded prospect."

"But for sure no *Lear.*"

"My dear fellow," Digby said.

"Meanwhile," Bender said, "'Twas brillig and the slithy toves for you."

"That or the ramen diet," Digby said. "Anything is better than not working."

The note on the business card Lucy handed him instructed him to be at the Scarlett Begonia restaurant in Victoria Court. "Nine a.m.," the note read. "Consider this an audition, as well as breakfast."

"It's from them," Lucy said. "They're making contact."

The card, printed on thick, linen-based stock, the printing itself raised, gave the impression of letterpress. The organization name, Epic Productions. A modest scroll carried the motto, "Make Your Productions Epic." Underneath, an address and zip code could have been in one of the older studios in East Hollywood.

The individual presented on the card was J.J. Dykstra. His title, Development Executive.

Bender arrived early. When shown to the table, he found his hosts already seated. *Think Rosencrantz and Guildenstern,* Bender told himself. *Think the two hired guns from Hemingway's story, "The Killers."* The one Digby'd described as tall and cadaverous stood to greet him. "Jay

Dykstra. Good to see you. This," he indicated the Falstaffian one, "is my colleague, Don Van Hirtum."

"Don't get up," Bender said.

"Wasn't going to," Van Hirtum said. "Making notes."

After a waitress poured coffee for them, Dykstra produced an iPad, which he set on the table. "Can we get some conversation from you, Matt? Okay to call you Matt?"

"Sure," Bender said. He motioned Dykstra to sit before he began. "Blow, winds, and crack your cheeks," he said. "Rage. Blow. You cataracts and hurricanes, spout. Till you have drench'd our steeples, drowned the cocks."

"Fuckin' Shakespeare," Van Hirtum told Dykstra. "*King Lear*. Act three, scene two."

"We were hoping for something more conversational," Dykstra said.

Van Hirtum produced an iPad of his own, scrolled through it until he arrived at what Bender reckoned to be a chart. "Low approval ratings," Van Hirtum said. "Does slightly better in the sixty-to-sixty-five age range, but definitely low approval in our target audience range."

"What are you talking about?"

"Shakespeare," Van Hirtum said.

"Whereas," Dykstra said. "Tell him, Don."

"We got you scored high in the eighteen-to-thirty-five range."

"What the fuck is this?" Bender said.

"Notice where he put the break," Van Hirtum told Dykstra. "Right after the *fuck*. Kids love that kind of nuance."

Dykstra gestured as though trying to tamp down excessive clothing in a suitcase. "If you'll indulge us for a moment," he said, "we can walk you through something. It could work out quite well for you."

"You have nothing to do with television, do you?" Bender said.

"He thinks we're film people," Van Hirtum told Dykstra.

"What the fuck are you?" Bender said. "And what the fuck am I doing here?"

"Tell him, Jay."

"I'm trying, Donnie."

"He's not buying," Van Hirtum said. "I'm offended he thinks we're film people."

"Take it easy, Donnie. Once he gets it, we're okay." He spread his hands before Bender. "Listen, Matt. Still okay to call you Matt? Listen. We're talking long-term here. You have a powerful gift. Not many can connect with an audience the way you do. Don't think we didn't notice. Must have cost you a bundle, studying acting with Sandy Meisner. But look at the results."

"I studied with Jeff Corey," Bender said.

"My bad," Dykstra said. "Your way of handling pressure suggests Meisner."

"You're losing him, Jay," Van Hirtum said. "Our stress interview's going sideways."

"Well fucking told," Bender stood. "I'm out of here." He stormed toward the entry aisle, where the hostess held up a hand to slow him. "Something wrong with the coffee, sir?"

Bender carried his irritation with his personal Rosencrantz and Guildenstern through the day, into his performance that evening. The actors portraying Nick and Honey reeled and staggered in his presence. After Act One, Bender heard Nita Dunbar, playing Honey, cry in her dressing room from the emotional intensity.

He felt his edge retreat with each successive curtain call. By the time he slid into the damp comfort of the night, he became his accustomed, depleted, self after a performance, tired, hungry, not at all sure which of the two had first call on his attention.

He'd left his car parked next to a light fixture, chosen as a landmark against post-performance vagueness. When he approached, What the hell? Stella, leaning against his Camry, spotlighted. "You were really something tonight," she said.

Her oversized field jacket, out-at-the-knees jeans, and abused running shoes tugged at him. "Thank you," he said.

"Take me home?"

"Sure." He opened the door for her.

"I mean your home."

"What about the sous chef?"

Stella snuggled a shoulder against him. "He's at my place, waiting. He says being in this play has made me even more desirable."

"I don't see where this goes."

A shudder trickled through Stella. "I can't stand it when he puts his hands on me."

"Aw, for Christ's sake, Stella. That's right out of *The Postman Always Rings Twice*. Cora and Frank."

"But I relate to Cora. Richie said it would play."

"Richie?"

"My acting coach. Richie Powers."

"Unbelievable. So you don't really have a sous chef?"

"Raoul is real enough, but the thing is—"

"What is the thing?"

"He's all about wanting me to have his children. He's got names picked for them." She squeezed his arm. "I don't want kids."

"He's gaming you. Can't you see that?"

"I want to go home with you."

"Not a good idea. Not a good idea at all."

"Is this anything like your chicken experience?"

"Worse by several degrees, Stella."

"You can call me Mitzi if you want."

After the cast meeting the next day, Digby motioned Bender to wait. He probed the depths of his safari jacket pockets to produce a familiar business card.

"Rosencrantz and Guildenstern strike back."

"Apparently with an act of contrition, which," he said, waving the card at Bender, "is the first step toward—"

"Okay." Bender took the card. "I get it. Absolution."

Digby shook his head. "Absolution, dear boy, is not for the likes of us. But perhaps a new job is. As the nurse said to the proctologist, when he withdrew a long-stemmed rosebud from the cavity of a patient, 'Read the card.'"

We got off on the wrong foot. Allow us to repair. Dunkin'. Four o'clock. Please!

Stella waited in the parking lot, dressed in a replay of last night. She'd either slept in those clothes or hadn't done enough laundry for a change. Didn't matter which—the effect hit him the same. Overcome by her vulnerability.

"I wanted you to know," she said. "I took your advice."

"I don't remember giving any."

"I sent him packing, Matt. I told him to take his things and go. I even made him take that humongous container of moo goo gai pan." She waited for a moment. "No more gaming. I've had it with gaming."

Stella showed no sign of leaving, even after Bender got into his Camry. "Chemistry." She leaned into his window. "You and me. We have good chemistry. Maybe you can't see it yet, but it's there."

He arrived earlier at Dunkin' Donuts than he'd expected. Once again, they were earlier. Dykstra saw him enter the driveway, tossed a cheery wave. Van Hirtum smiled.

When he reached their table, he saw they'd ordered for him. "Latte, right?" Dykstra said.

"Whole milk," Van Hirtum said.

"You have that on your iPads, do you?"

"Please," Dykstra said. "Can we forget last time? Instead, let's get to the point of our interest in you and the prospects we're authorized to offer on behalf of our client."

Made Bender think, "Who was that masked man?" Instead, he said, "Who is this client of yours?"

Van Hirtum pointed to Bender's coffee, invited him to sip, pushed a large tray of crullers toward him.

"Donny here loves the Dunkin' cruller," Dykstra said. "He thought you might enjoy a few."

"Understand," Van Hirtum said. "We're not implying you're a cheap date." He hefted a cruller, took a bite of it. "I get such a kick out of these. Wanted to—"

"—share," Dykstra said.

"—share," Van Hirtum said.

"Your client?" Bender said. "Let's stick with that." He had the impression Dykstra fought back an impulse to offer a friendly arm pat, could see conflicting impulses in a struggle to produce companionability.

"The question, Jay," Van Hirtum said. "You gotta ask him the question. We gotta do this."

"Okay, "Dykstra said. "Okay. Please indulge us, Matt. No matter how you answer this question, we'll tell you who the client is and the potential for your future with this client."

Bender took a sip of his latte.

"May I take that as a yes?" Dykstra said.

"Go ahead," Bender said.

"We're given to understand," Dykstra began, "that you had some unfortunate past associations with—"

"—regarding," Van Hirtum said.

"Yes," Dykstra said. "Regarding. "

"Regarding?" Bender said.

"Chicken," Dykstra said.

Bender set down his latte. "That was six years ago."

"Five," Van Hirtum said. "New Orleans. The Rebellious Chicken."

"You have that in your iPad, do you?"

"Only as a talking point."

Bender stood. "If you have any knowledge of New Orleans temperature and humidity, you will appreciate how July is not a good time to wear any close-fitting costume, least of all a chicken costume."

"Okay," Dykstra said. "Thank you for your—"

"—honesty and cooperation," Van Hirtum said. "We get it. It was uncomfortable for you."

"Fucking traumatic," Bender said. "I never want to feel that claustrophobia again."

Van Hirtum motioned for him to sit.

Bender remained standing.

"Are you at all familiar," Dykstra said, "with the name Chick 'n' Waf?"

"From Seattle to San Diego," Van Hirtum said.

"No," Bender said. "Absolutely not."

"Soon to go national," he said. "Like next month."

"No," Bender said.

Dykstra's attempt to sing this like a jingle sounded conspiratorial. "Live it up with Chick 'n' Waf."

"No," Bender said.

"Spokesperson," Dykstra said. "Yearly stipend."

"No," Bender said.

"Only an hour at a time in each locale. Whole new technology in costumes. Breathable fabrics."

"I'm leaving now," Bender said.

"Filmed spots. In-studio. You and the Waffle, sometimes in conversation. Your faces fully visible," Dykstra said.

"Residuals," Van Hirtum said. "You could build up quite a nest egg."

"Humorous exchanges, literary and historical allusions."

"Faces?" Bender said. "Faces? "

"You and the Waffle, of course."

"Let me guess," Bender said. "Stella?"

"Great chemistry between you," Dykstra said. "Unmistakable."

"Absolutely not," Bender said.

Before the performance that night, Stella sat in his dressing room, made up as Martha. "Do you have any idea what this means to me?" she said. "Of course you don't. You get people from Hollywood in the audience. All I get? Older men, wanting to sponsor me. Do you know what sponsor means?"

Bender sighed. "I know what sponsor means. I thought we agreed to quit with the Cora stuff."

"Be that as it may," Stella said. "I couldn't be in this play, working with a director like Digby, and actors like you and Nita and Louie without having a union card. You take the union for granted. I understand how desperate Cora felt. Even though she's only a character, she knew what she had to do to get things."

"Five minutes," Digby said through the door.

"I need you to go," Bender said.

"I don't see how you can walk away from this. I know you can, but I wish you could explain it to me. I really feel the chemistry. For the first time. I've never got makeup or sweat in my eye from the stage lights before. I've never been this far in. Working with you, I can feel it."

"Please," Bender told Stella. "Please go."

"I'd like to understand," Stella said.

Bender froze when he heard his name called. Who would know him here? Like the sting from drinking ice water too fast. "Matt Bender? That's you, isn't it?"

Fucking Digby.

"I recognize the way you walk," Digby said.

"What are you doing here?" Bender said.

"The Fresno High School Warriors want a new drama instructor. I'm here to—"

"Audition," Bender said. He tugged at his chicken-head helmet, lifted it, blinked in the sharp San Joaquin Valley light. "'Now mark me,'" he said, "'how I will undo myself. I give this heavy weight from off my head.'"

"My dear fellow," Digby said. "Richard the Second. Giving up his crown."

Bender pointed to a nearby metal-and-glass building, framed by fluttering yellow and blue pennants and the larger Welcome to the Fresno Chick 'n' Waf banner. A figure stepped away from a clamoring group of patrons, began an energetic wave of arms in their direction.

What on earth is that?" Digby asked.

"Peer awareness," Bender said. "The Waffle recognizes you."

BLOOD MOON

by Chella Courington

Sophie tickles my cheek with her tongue to attract me, and I give her my right arm. Like the Virgin's mantle sliding over my shoulder, she rolls her muscles to the drummer's heartbeat, washing me in light. Mama calls my boa a serpent, and me a "dirty coochie dancer. Jesus is in covered-dish suppers at the Boaz Baptist Church." But I believe he's in Sophie. At the Bottoms Up Bar she first appeared—eyes milky, scales ghost white. Just slept on a cover under the sink and refused to eat for six days. On the seventh, clouds evaporated. Clear dark eyes and bright brown body. Three days later, she rubbed and pushed her nose against the back screen until the skin broke. All day she pressed against the linoleum floor, never letting up. At night a translucent ribbon lay on the quilt—eye caps on top.

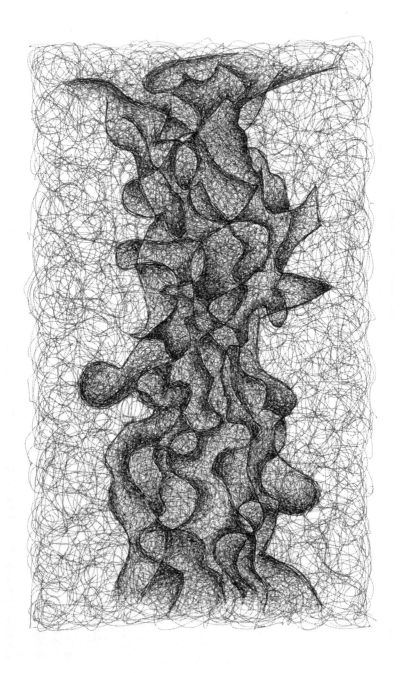

"Untitled September 28, 2015" by Stephen T. Vessels

DRY RUN FOR DOOMSDAY

by Max Talley

The house shuddered. Throbbing vibrations from low-flying helicopters woke Marcus Dahlgren. He felt as if he'd been asleep for days, the Southern California storms that raged since Sunday finally subsiding. Darkness everywhere; the power flickered on and off in his bedroom. Padding into the living room, Marcus discovered the lamps worked but electricity had been off. The clock blinked 2:37 a.m. despite the gray light seeping through the blinds suggesting it was after dawn.

Marcus charged his iPhone and the print read 19:45. *What the hell?* It had never shown military time before. Next, he couldn't access his e-mail. The phone's screen kept flashing a "Settings Update?" balloon. When he pressed "Not Now," the notice reappeared. When he pressed "Update," nothing happened. Instead, he checked his texts. Ten messages, but not a single number he recognized.

My husband heard about us. Be careful, you know how violent he can be.
You owe $463.27 in unpaid bills—SoCal Gas.
It's Rachel. I saw what you posted. You'll suffer for this.
Te amo, querida—Rolando.

Absurd. Marcus powered up his laptop. Fuzzy static showed, blinking images, the computer struggling to reach clarity. He clicked on Firefox and the screen went black with large white sentences forming across it in Cyrillic script. Other sections looked Arabic. The browser wouldn't function so Marcus squinted at the indecipherable words.

Was this the fucking Dark Web he'd heard about? Some evil Internet where terrorists and Russian trolls did their dirty work in an untraceable void? Finally the screen went blank, but Marcus powered off when the computer felt hot. *Has to be some glitch.* A major satellite went down, or weather interference. Conspiracy theorists had predicted such chaos.

A framed photograph of Octavia sat atop his desk. Three years up in Seattle. She definitely wasn't coming back. Marcus opened his front door to peer through the hooked screen door at the neighbors he never spoke to as they packed a tent and sleeping bags into their Ford Explorer. Today seemed an odd time for a camping trip.

Out in the misty, wet air, no one walked dogs or jogged along the damp sidewalks. Marcus heard sirens in the distance but didn't feel concerned. In Santa Valeria, a third of the population were seniors, so 911 calls happened most days. Ambulance. Fire engine. Police car.

Marcus remained enthralled by the ashtray sky and an advancing column of ominous clouds until banging on the door's frame startled him.

"Hello, mister?" a squeaky voice said. A little boy, maybe four or five, pressed his face to the screen.

"Are you the noisy kid from across the street?"

"Let me in," the child said. "My house is dark. My mommy and daddy are gone."

Marcus unhooked the door. "Why aren't you in preschool?"

"Because of rain and stuff." The boy dashed inside. "My name is Zayden. Got any cookies?"

"Zayden? That's a weird name."

"No it isn't," the boy said. "You're weird, and you're funny looking."

Marcus exhaled. "Let's see if I have any snacks." When he returned with milk and banana bread, Zayden had cast off his shirt.

"I want to take a bath."

"Are you crazy? No kid wants to take a bath."

"The water in my house is brown, like doody." Zayden darted past Marcus into the bedroom.

Marcus set the plate and glass down and followed.

The child attempted to remove his pants.

An undressed little boy in a middle-aged bachelor's place? "Jesus Christ," Marcus yelled. With a superhuman surge of adrenaline, Marcus pulled the kid's pants back up, lifted him in the air, somehow got the guy into his shirt and tiny shoes, then carried him outside. "Go home and wait for your parents, Zayden."

The boy scurried across the street to a stucco house.

Marcus turned on the bathroom sink faucet and brown water exploded out—as if under immense pressure. Using bottled water in a salad bowl, Marcus brushed his teeth and shaved, but had to substitute a shower with a French bath. *Is that PC to say anymore?* he wondered.

Although disoriented, Marcus thought it best to go to work—even if he was late.

Standing on the brick stairway that formed his small landing, Marcus noticed a garbage truck churning and groaning out on Palm Street. However, when the green-vested man came wheeling a beige bin, he unloaded bulging plastic bags from it and deposited them into the empty trash cans outside Marcus's cottage.

"Hey, what's going on?"

The worker put a finger to his lips to shush Marcus. "We're returning all garbage until further notice." The man hustled away, rolling the tilted bin through dirty puddles.

Marcus tucked into his 1999 Honda Civic and drove west toward Main Street, intending to turn north to his office. A mass of idling cars greeted him; a roadblock loomed ahead. "Oh, shit." Intersection signals blinked red lights. More fucking power outages.

A man in a hard hat and orange vest strode down the line, peering in car windows and barking commands. "You need to turn around," he told Marcus. "Main Street and access west are blocked until further notice."

"But my job..."

"Not today. The west side of Santa Valeria has been evacuated."

"Why?"

"The Federal Government no longer allows us to

disclose information on environmental issues." The man extended his hands palms up.

"So flooding from storms affected power lines?"

"Please, sir." The man frowned. "We've all had a really long day."

"Sure, okay. But is it morning or afternoon?"

"Yes," the man replied. He scrambled toward the next car.

Marcus did a u-turn and called the InfoTech office. His phone worked outside. "Hey, Jenny, can you tell Brad I'm delayed getting in today with the crazy stuff going on?"

An interstice of silence, then, "Marcus, this is Brad. Stay home. Keep working on putting customers from various files into one master list doc, okay?"

"That's super-easy. I can probably find a way around the roadblock."

"Take the rest of the week off."

Marcus parked. "Really, why?"

"It came down from the top. Everyone but management."

"Uh, all right," Marcus said.

"By the way, how's Octavia doing?"

"She's still in Seattle."

"That's great you guys can make long distance work."

"She left me..."

"Oh." Brad cleared his throat. "Anyway, be safe."

When Marcus called, Southern California Edison played a recording: "We are experiencing power outages. Crews are working in your area and we expect this to be resolved by-by-by..." The message stuttered until the line disconnected.

Marcus drove south toward Ocean View Boulevard to

detour around the blockade. However, an Amtrak train lay stalled across his route, and it stretched to the neighboring streets as well—preventing coastline access. Frustrated, Marcus cruised back to Palm Street and texted friends. No one responded. He reclined the Honda's driver's seat, closing his eyes. A sharp tapping on the car window surprised him awake.

"Hey, Marcus," a raspy female voice said. An abundance of freckled, sun-burned cleavage heaved up into view. "Long time no see."

Marcus gazed up at a woman with messy blonde hair framing a face that showed serious road wear. She wore the tight, revealing clothing of someone much younger.

"Don't you remember me?"

"Leanne?" He squinted. "It's been ten years."

"Today's your lucky day." She smiled. "Listen, I need somewhere to crash until this whole shit-show ends. Been evacuated. Your place is on higher ground."

"So it was a flood?"

"The rains, and apparently a minor tsunami from a Japanese earthquake."

"Wow. I guess you can stay on the couch."

"Great," she said. "Don't expect anything else though."

"I don't."

"Right." She cackled. "Come on, this damp weather makes my bones ache." Leanne lumbered toward his cottage, carrying a packed laundry bag. Inside, she plunked down on the couch and lit a Marlboro.

"Do you know what time it is?"

Leanne checked her Samsung phone. "Almost five."

Marcus studied her. "Got Internet?"

"Nope." She looked up. "You ever been to the Cherry Pit?"

"The dive bar? You still drinking?"

"Not anymore." Leanne put her phone down. "Anyway, I'm there and this crusty dude says he's Uncle Vick, wants to buy me another Shirley Temple. I say, you're old enough to be my father. He says, no, he's old enough to be my uncle. Can you believe that?"

Marcus regretted agreeing to let her stay.

"So Uncle Vick hits on me," Leanne continued. "Of course I turned him down. I mean, not the first times, but by the third night at his house I said, enough is enough. I mean, I don't have to tell you that being an alcoholic doesn't exactly help a man in the sack."

"Uh, you were the drinker," Marcus said, "and we fooled around once, but you passed out, so nothing happened."

"Thanks for mansplaining. But what I remember is—"

"Listen, you can only stay tonight. My, uh, sister is visiting tomorrow."

"Seriously? Jesus. Okay, whatever." Leanne stamped through the kitchen. "Let's head down to The Pit after my nap." She locked his bedroom door behind her.

Marcus searched for news but his flat screen showed only static. His computer wouldn't log onto the Internet and his iPhone had locked displaying the wrong time, 23:17.

Then the power died.

They strolled the half mile south as dusk deepened into evening. Street lights were extinguished and yellowy candle light flickered in house windows. Some residents sat on porches with Coleman lanterns, waiting for Southern California Edison, for resolution. A constant whoosh and thrum of engines sounded on Highway 101 in the distance, but local streets seemed void of car traffic. The loamy smells of nature after a storm suffused the air.

"It's so quiet," Leanne whispered. "Kind of nice." Her neck cricked as she turned. "Want to hold my hand?"

"That's okay." Marcus smiled.

"Dick."

Marcus stared upward as they continued trekking, but couldn't see any stars or moon—eclipsed by darkness. Out of nowhere, three fighter jets came shrieking past them, flying low overhead before angling toward Los Angeles.

They both ducked as the ground trembled.

"Damn," Leanne said. "What a way to harsh my buzz."

"I thought you were sober now."

"I am. Weed, dude."

The Cherry Pit was illuminated by candles and hanging construction work lights. A generator yammered incessantly outside. The main room had a bar to the right, with a pool table and jukebox on the left. Through a set of curtains were rest rooms, a small lounge area, then a fenced-in patio for smokers, and where Marcus heard that regulars dealt weed and opioids.

An older, bearded man wearing a nautical hat approached.

"There he is," Leanne said, grinning. "Good to see you, slugger."

"Uncle Vick?" Marcus asked.

The man frowned and Leanne elbowed Marcus.

"This is Captain Jack," Leanne announced, as if common knowledge.

"Join me for a warm beer, babe," Captain Jack said.

"Aren't you on the wagon?" Marcus whispered.

"I'm not an alcoholic," Leanne insisted. "I drink by choice."

Marcus followed as she wedged in between people massed at the bar, but Leanne turned to shove him back a step. "My plans just changed. I'll come get my stuff tomorrow." She gave Marcus a please-go-away-now smile. "Thanks, dude."

He drifted to the back room. At a corner table under dim Christmas lights, Marcus saw a familiar face.

"Hey, Brad. What are you..." As Marcus got closer, the man turned. He wore an eye-patch and a scar ran across his forehead.

"Brad? My name's Dent."

"Sorry, my mistake."

"People often think I'm someone else," Dent said. "Wonder if the Brads of the world get mistaken for me?"

"Don't know." Marcus shrugged.

"Well, come join us. Nothing to do but wait out the incident."

"Incident?" Marcus sat down next to a fortyish Japanese-American woman, who swayed back and forth, and another man whose head lay atop his folded arms on the table.

"We've been here since noon," Dent said in explanation.

Marcus nodded. "So it's a flood from the rain and a minor tsunami?"

"Could be an attack," Dent said. "I mean, look how unstable things are in Washington." Using both hands, Dent pushed at his facial flesh as if trying to give himself a facelift.

"F-16s and helicopters been flying overhead all day. Never a good sign."

"No, feels like a dress rehearsal for doomsday."

The slumbering man levered his head upwards. "Massive power outages in San Diego and rumors of an explosion in the LADWP power plant. Hills are on fire along the 405." He scowled. "We had sporadic electricity until late afternoon."

"Thanks, Garth," Dent said. "But that doesn't account for the other weird stuff."

"Nope." Garth pressed his greasy, graying hair back. "Best case scenario: winds knocked power lines down. Worst case: cyber-attack or a North Korean missile."

"Before he got dismissed, Garth taught philosophy at UCLA."

"I wouldn't want to be in L.A. now." Garth's eyes went wide. "A mass of refugees heading northward. And we're only ninety miles farther up the coast."

"Refugees?" Dent said. "Pure speculation. You're drunk."

"Maybe." Garth exhaled. "People wait a day or two before panicking and fleeing, then it's too late."

Marcus leaned in. "What are you talking about?"

"Disaster movies," Garth said. "I've seen them all. Every scenario."

Marcus asked Dent, "Why the barricades?"

"Could be flooding," he replied. "Or to secure the banks from break-ins."

"There's been a coup." Garth banged his fist on the table. "Started after JFK was assassinated..."

The woman laughed.

"You mean LBJ is to blame for this?" Marcus half-smiled.

"The coup took over fifty years to reach fruition," Garth said, resting his head on the drowsy woman's shoulder. "But in the measure of cosmic time, that's like a nanosecond, man."

Dent staggered toward the rest rooms.

"I haven't been on Facebook in over twelve hours," the woman said, her body trembling. "Can't take it anymore."

"Don't you see," Garth continued. "America and Russia used to be enemies but that Cold War kept us all alive. Now our clown and their thug are planning a lovers' leap together into the apocalypse."

"That's lovely," Marcus said, "but what's Dent's story?"

Garth wiped his sweaty face with a shirt sleeve. "Doctor Denton, best Lasik surgeon in town until he got hooked on Percocet after a mountain-biking accident. Affected him mentally. He performed Lasik surgery on himself. Went horribly wrong, as you can see by the eye patch." Garth sighed.

The woman suddenly straightened up. "This is like that Townes Van Zandt song. We're sitting around waiting to die." She closed her eyes and leaned her head back against the wall.

"I have to get to Humboldt County," Garth said.

"Why?" Marcus asked.

"Oregon or Washington would be safer. But if the shit hits the fan, I want to be stoned out of my gourd on Humboldt green bud. Won't feel a thing."

The woman sighed. "You're such an idiot."

"Need to leave tonight. Highways will be jammed tomorrow."

"Great talking to you," Marcus said, "but I have a

friend up front."

He needed fresh air. The patio had emptied besides a college-aged, alluring black woman picking up empty beer bottles. Reminded Marcus of someone. With back lighting from a tiki torch casting a halo over her frizz of tight curls, she looked angelic, worthy of stained glass.

"Could you save me?" Marcus asked.

"What? For real?"

"For real."

She smirked. "I've got nothing, especially for an old white dude."

"I'm forty-six."

"Perspective. My ten-year-old cousin thinks I'm old."

"I feel lost, adrift in my life."

She continued collecting glasses. "You're like a guy on the railing of the *Titanic*. You're searching for anything floating by to jump onto." She sighed into a sad laugh. "See my job? Where I work? I'm not a lifeboat, I'm an ashtray."

"Sorry." Marcus retreated.

The generator had stopped, leaving the barroom dark and noisy. He didn't find Leanne at the bar and didn't particularly care. Instead, Marcus slipped through the crowd to gaze at the starless sky outside. Distant sirens wailed.

Someone grabbed him from behind.

"Take me with you," Garth said.

"I'm heading home."

"Take me, please." Garth held onto his shoulder.

"Look, I'm flattered, really, but I'm just not that into you."

"Jesus, no, man. Take me on your escape plan. I read your eyes. You have one worked out. I'll pitch in gas money, plus help scrounge for supplies."

"Get a hold of yourself." Marcus detached himself from Garth's grip. "I'm going to get some sleep. When we wake up, this will all be sorted out."

"What if it isn't?"

"Then by afternoon or evening." Marcus took a deep breath. "We're in California, the sixth biggest economy in the world."

"Don't give me that happy horseshit." Garth's face looked strained, grotesque. "You drank the Kool-Aid, you're already dead."

Garth launched into him and they fell onto moist grass. The drunk took some swings but they landed like limp slaps. Marcus kicked the fool backward. Garth picked himself up off the sidewalk and flapped a hand at Marcus in disgust before shuffling back inside the Cherry Pit.

This isn't a Third World country, Marcus thought. *It'll be resolved. Today will seem like a bad dream tomorrow.*

Marcus walked up the gradual slope of San Pablo Street, hearing dogs barking to the west, followed by a lone coyote's dissonant howl from the northern foothills, and he strolled past an older couple with questioning faces, so he shook his head in answer. Hispanic chefs and busboys spoke rapid Spanish outside a closed Mexican restaurant. Marcus moved beyond them and the mute millennials on street corners, who stared at their useless phones, and after crossing Monterey Avenue—where displaced homeless people camped in the park by a school—he finally reached Palm Street.

Marcus navigated his cottage using a flashlight. He felt a strange clarity, the air charged with positive ions. Setting Leanne's heavy laundry bag outside on the landing, Marcus tied the straps to his screen door handle. He packed clothes, along with Trader Joe's bagels and the remaining banana bread, then lugged a plastic gallon container of water to his Honda.

A block away, the closed school played relaxing Japanese koto music over their outdoor PA system. They had a back-up generator. Marcus imagined a red Facebook meme: *Keep calm and run for your fucking life.*

He took the Garcia Street on-ramp to Highway 101 North and merged into the flow. The three lanes were filled with people driving a steady thirty mph. CHP cars flashed on the median and clear zone, blocking maniacs from illegally speeding around. Stern officers waved drivers onward. Traffic stood at a standstill on the southbound side, emergency vehicles occasionally forcing themselves through with a wail of sirens and a strobe of lights.

The dashboard digital clock showed 12:10, and Marcus felt confident he could make Salinas by dawn. His fuel gauge needle sat at a half-tank. If today turned out to be just a glitch, a weekend up north wouldn't kill him. If not, Humboldt County then Oregon sounded like fine destinations. Things would have to be truly severe to justify driving to Seattle.

Only darkness and an endless snake of headlights showed in his rear view mirror.

NIGHT MUST WAIT

by Robin Winter

Dense green *Clerodendrum* cascaded from the trellis against the wall of the house. Wilton looked past the trimmed bush of Yesterday Today and Tomorrow flowers, in their three colors from intense violet to pallid drooping white. She saw that no one stood near enough to watch what she did. Of course she was safe, in an enclosed garden with guards at the walls.

Straight from God. There he was, sleek, twice the length of her arm, moving along the thick branch of the tree. His lidless eye fixed. He paused, forked tongue flickering, tasting her on the air.

She clutched her pillowcase which lay slack across her knees, empty. When she started to move, she held it in her left fist and stood. She reached with boneless grace. To capture a snake you must become like him, fluid motion.

Predator against predator. How sweet, how soft. Her hand stroked up the long limb of the cashew tree and ran a light touch over the smooth head of the black cobra before sliding around his throat. Then a firm grip, a practiced gesture. The snake strained back with powerful muscles, but her fingers did not give.

She dropped the case and with her other hand unwound the lithe form from its place. It had eaten recently, a slight bulge attesting to the death of a mouse or lizard. Wilton settled the snake deep in her pillowcase, slow and careful, the snake too valuable for haste. It did not strike at the fabric when she slipped her grip loose and drew her fingers back along the curve of neck until she could withdraw her hand. She twisted the top tight and picked up the bag full of snake, supporting the weight in her arms. It settled deep with a whispered hiss.

THE RUNE MAKER AND
THE RIVER PYTHON

by Cyrus Cromwell

The following is an excerpt of Cyrus Cromwell's novel, Born of Fire, *Book I of the* Shadow Dragons Trilogy. *Young Will, an orphan of Asharad, has fought a sand fiend in the desert and earned a spot as a fledgling dragon rider of Aeronoth. He has survived many initiations with his dragon, Keoria, as war and danger brew in the Vale he seeks to protect.*

The clear blue sky stretched out in an endless vista around Will and Keoria as they glided through the whispering clouds of mid-day sky. Even on the way to the Stone King they had not flown this high. Will noted the sun was sharper at this height, yet the wind passing through him was icy cold. The silence was just as much a revelation as ever, marked only by the sound of Keoria's wings and the low thrum of fire in her core. Both dragon and rider were content in the silence of the moment.

Dragon riders of Aeronoth rarely had cause to fly this far Westward, past the vast stretch of the Ranghorn Forest. Two days prior they had passed the western defenses of the Vale, the network of stone walls and towers and the vigilant horsemen that patrolled its lengths. Staying silent and high; unnoticed on a trip that needed no questions asked.

After the previous nine months at Aeronoth, so filled with people and activity, this sojourn was already a blissful respite. There was something pure and elemental about flying at such a great height, and as the clouds snaked past, Will realized that he had already begun to understand the path of the dragon rider—the resonance between rider and dragon, dragon and the world in its rawest form. It occurred to him that here he was at tremendous heights and yet he felt no fear of falling from Keoria, as if such an incongruence was utterly impossible.

Such is the way of the dragon rider, he thought.

Keoria blew short flames through her nostrils in acknowledgement and began a slow descent. *Even from up here the river looks big,* thought Will.

Bright sunlight danced and sparkled off the serpentine pathways of the Eridin River. Cutting through the Ranghorn Forest, the river moved North to South in a not particularly direct fashion, as if a child of the gods had thrown a ball of silver string into the air just to see how it might land.

As the river exited the southern end of the forest it wrapped around the base of a barren volcanic mountain, risen in lonely fashion, yet with trees lined right up to its base on the one side, as if it were the adopted sentinel of the southern entrance to the forest realm.

There it is, Will, the Southern Cauldron. The Fei-Kannere camp is at the base of it on the river side.

Let's stay high until they give us a sign, replied Will.

As Will said so, a whistling sound and arcing display of light in the form of a dragon talisman broached the sky directly above the slope of the mountain. *Always nice to get a welcome, mused Keoria.*

Indeed it is, replied Will with a smile.

Keoria took a slow arc around the side of the mountain and landed easily beneath the remnants of the floating dragon pendant.

A black-haired woman in a white robe approached them as they landed and cast her gaze over them both.

"Welcome grand red and dragon rider," she announced. "I am Melthusa. The Warlock has been expecting you, Will. He is very interested to meet you."

The woman stepped forward and placed her hand softly on the side of Keoria's face.

"Keoria, you are free to join their meeting if it pleases you, or you may partake of our lava steam chambers. You are welcome to go wherever you wish here or in the village. We are worshippers of the Earth Fire here and your visit is quite an honor."

The honor is mine, Melthusa, replied Keoria. *I know of your family lineage. Your line has always been close to the dragon spirit. There is still much light left in the day, I would be pleased to take you for a ride if you so desire.*

"I would like that very much," she replied.

Melthusa turned to address Will as he released from

the saddle. "The middle opening is the one you want." As she spoke, she gestured to a series of three white fabric outcroppings raised as entrances into the side of the mountain. With that, she slid onto Keoria's saddle and the two flew into the sky.

The three outcroppings were made of heavy linen, with leather trim and bindings holding them tight to strong wooden poles inserted into the mountainside. Will took a second to consider them. These constructions were not totally inanimate. He felt an essence emanating from them, an intangible quality he could not describe in words, but that he knew well enough by now. These entrances were protected by powerful magical wards, and it was unlikely that even an insect of unwanted origin would be able to pass through them.

Will stepped up to the center entrance and watched as the linen flaps softened and parted, an invitation to come deeper into the mountain. Will took a breath and stepped inside.

A few minutes later, Will found himself sitting in front of Malik the Warlock, who was a tapestry of extremes: thick black hair over impossibly white skin, white sashes intersecting with the lines of his royal red robe. He was tall and robust, somehow hardy and ethereal at the same time.

"I trust the heat is not too overwhelming for you?" asked the Warlock.

"I spend my mornings in a forge. I live for the heat, the fire, and the steel," replied Will.

"That is good. I too, understand the fire and the heat. Tell me young Will of Aeronoth, what prompted you to contact me?"

"I am still learning the ways of magic, but I understand

it's best not to show up unannounced on a warlock's doorstep. And, while you and I are friends of the fire, not everyone is as accommodating of dragons."

"True enough, on both counts," replied the warlock. "But you didn't answer my question. You are here because you are seeking something. What is it that you seek?"

"I seek to transform this..." Will gestured at the side of his neck and pulled his arm out of his tunic showing the full length of the scarring over his shoulder and arm.

"That is an interesting choice of words," replied Malik. "Transform. I take it you said it that way on purpose, which implies that you do not mean to get rid of it."

"Correct," replied Will. "I want to give it a different meaning. I want to turn it into something other than a scar. I want to turn it into something to be proud of. I want you to engrave a rune into it."

The warlock tapped his fingers together in front of him as he contemplated Will's request.

"You wish to take something that was done to you and turn it into something purposeful. And you think a rune will do this for you. Interesting. Tell me, young Will, how did you come by this scar?"

At this prompting, Will related the story of the sand fiend attack in the desert and the events that followed. When Will finished, the Warlock sat back in his chair and gave Will a thoughtful yet intense look.

"The scar you seek to mark. It got you into Aeronoth, when you previously had no future and no prospects. It made you a dragon rider. It led you to Keoria. It has kept you company in the Forge at Aeronoth. It has been there every time you struck hammer to steel and every time you threw yourself into the dragon's saddle. A mark, given to you by one of the largest and most powerful creatures known, a creature born and made of the deepest earth. This mark makes you different. It is the most important and powerful thing about you. Yet, you do not value it because you did not have control over how it came to you? That is hubris. That is pride."

Will was stunned. He had not expected this rebuke.

The warlock pursed his lips. "To mark your scar with a rune under that pretext would be folly. Without a doubt, the magic would not hold and would instead rebel. Or it would condemn you to a life of rejecting your own self. You would be nothing but a wandering wraith. Regretfully, I can not accommodate your request. I do appreciate your visit, however. Please stay the night and enjoy our hospitality. There is always room among the Fei-Kannere for dragons and their riders."

The warlock clapped his hands and two servants appeared, dressed similarly in white and red.

"Brex and Heron will show you to the guest quarters, young rider."

Will rose, still in shock, and followed the pair out of the warlock's chambers.

As the daytime progressed into the evening hours, a grand party was constructed along the base of the mountain where Keoria and Will had landed hours earlier. Poles of fire-treated wood were erected with strings of flowers and vines connecting them. Lanterns of magical firelight were hung from the boughs. Many mighty oak tables were laid out and all manner of food and drink prepared.

For all his consternation at the words of the warlock earlier, Will found himself caught up in the festivities. Dancing and merriment intertwined with stories of the Fei-Kannere and stories of sand fiends and orcs.

Keoria had come back from her flight with Melthusa to discover the joys of the lava steam chambers. Buried within the mountain, these large caves had rocks super-heated by the lava, and the Fei-Kannere had built stone tunnels to divert river water over the rocks, creating steam chambers for healing and relaxation. Keoria had been escorted to the one chamber big enough to hold a dragon and had quickly made herself at home. She too was enjoying festivities, resting at the edge of the encampment, and blowing smoke rings from her nostrils for the local children.

Will took a seat up against Keoria's side. *Malik refuses to mark my scar with a rune.*

So I heard.

You seem unconcerned. It is the whole reason we came here.

He is a warlock, replied Keoria. *Living here with the Fei-Kannere is clearly, shall we say, just one aspect of the man. According to Melthusa, he is wise and capable of a great many things. If he chooses to not mark you with a rune, I trust his judgement.*

But he's telling me that I've been deluded, fooling myself for the last year, replied Will.

Keoria chuckled and slightly shifted her weight.

I would say that hardly makes you any different from the rest of your race. As near as I can tell, the lot of you see the world the way you want to see it, and you believe whatever fits into the view of the world you already have.

Oh great, replied Will, *Now you have it out for me too.*

Not likely. I have no reason to. Humans make themselves miserable wallowing between what they expect to be and what is. You expect a certain outcome and when the world doesn't give you that, you experience great upset and commotion.

Will sat silent for a moment and gave an exasperated exhale. *I suppose I can't really argue with anything you just said.*

Of course not, replied Keoria with a smoky laugh.

Will looked up at the stars for a moment and before long he was fast asleep laying against Keoria's side.

The early sun woke Will the next morning, its soft light streaking through air permeated by the vitality and energy of the surrounding forest. Still laying on the ground against Keoria's side, he took a moment to ponder the events of the night before. His mind returned to the matter of the rune. It had drawn him here. And now, even after the warlock's rejection, it would not let him go.

Only one thing to do, thought Will to himself as he rose from the ground.

He made his way to the entrance of the Warlock's tunnels and found the flowing linen swaying gently aside for him. After heading a short distance down the tunnel to the Warlock's receiving room he was just a little surprised to see the Warlock dressed and groomed at this table, looking for all the world as if he was expecting Will's company.

Malik turned to fully face Will. "Warlocks make it a habit to never be surprised. Please, have a seat."

Will followed Malik's gesturing arm and took a seat in the same guest chair he had sat in the day before.

"So you knew why I was coming here?" asked Will.

"Of course," replied the Warlock.

"If you don't mind me asking, what are you doing here?" asked Will in a friendly tone.

"Awaiting your arrival this morning, of course," replied the Warlock in a bemused tone.

"I mean, what are you doing here with the Fei-Kannere, living in the mountain?"

"Why does anyone live anywhere?" came the answer, complete with cocked head and curious expression.

"You're a warlock. Which means, by definition, you are not just anyone. You chose to be here and I'm guessing for a very specific reason."

The Warlock paused a moment and held Will with a direct gaze. "That is as dangerous a question as you can ask a Warlock. However, since you had the courage to ask it, I will tell you. Quite simply, I am here with the Earth Fire, building power."

Will pondered that for a long moment.

"I understand what you mean because I am doing the same thing at Aeronoth," responded Will. "Building power, somehow seeping into me from the walls of Aeronoth, from the books, from the Forge, from every time I saddle up on Keoria and feel the fire in her core. That's real and that's true.

I've been laboring under a burden of my own making with my scar, as if I was looking for something to hold me back. I took a gift and made it my enemy, a throne of pity to sit in front of and convince myself that I was nothing. Before I joined that caravan in the desert, that's all I had heard from anyone, that I was nothing. And you're right, if it weren't for the sand fiend, I'd be back in Asharad, or some place just like it, busy in the alleyways trying to find coin and drink.

"Last night I talked with Keoria into the late hours and I've decided to change how I hold this in my mind. From here forward I am going to own my experience with the sand fiend, be proud that I acted like a soldier should and that I have this reminder of my heroism marking my body. I came here looking for a rune. Now I realize I already have one. I want to thank you for that gift. Thank you also for your hospitality. Keoria and I will be airborne and back to the Vale within the hour."

Malik sat back in his chair, his fingertips tapping together in front of him.

"Understanding true power is the journey of a lifetime, young Will. You are taking the first steps. Simply by the realization you just shared with me, you are moving closer to the natural accord of events, closer to dragon consciousness, and closer to the earth. That is quite a change from the fellow I talked to yesterday. With that mindset, I will mark you with a rune. A second rune, to add power to the one you already have."

Malik snapped his finger and his two attendants entered the receiving chamber a few moments later.

"Is the Chamber of Marking ready?" he asked.

"All is as you requested master," came their reply.

Malik turned back to Will. "There is one further step you must take to prepare yourself for the marking. You must cleanse yourself in the river. The magic works best if you are free of whatever you have been carrying. The river helps with that."

One of the attendants stepped forward with a long cloth and a change of clothes—simple beige linen, yet marked with a cascade of magical symbols.

"Cleanse yourself. Put on the ritual clothing. Then make your way back here," explained the warlock.

Will nodded his head in agreement, took the clothing and headed out of the mountain.

The path to the river was easily accessible and Will was quickly on his way. The morning air was warm and moist, not something Will was used to from Aeronoth or Asharad. He made his way down through the relatively lush forest trail to the edge of the riverbank. He arrived at a small but hospitable crescent of sand gliding into a calm slice of the river protected from the greater flow by a jetty of underwater rocks. Will undressed in the warm morning air and hung his clothes from one of the nearby branches.

"Time to get cleansed," he muttered to himself as he stepped into the water. It was cold but not unmanageably so and Will quickly found himself both awake and enjoying the coolness of the water. The bend in the river prior to this eddy was graced by streaks of grey and white rock covered with rich black dirt and a great many trees reaching out over the water. Will found himself drinking in the nature as he walked deeper on the sandy bottom. Up to his chest in the water he plunged his head beneath and felt the sweat of the flight, the conversation with the warlock, and the festivities of the night before wash easily from his body.

Will came up for air and let out a whoop of excitement. Somehow it felt like the heat and intensity of the desert and the Stone King and the orcs washed out of him—carried off by the river. Will let out a long exhale. As he did so, he noticed that the sash from the new set of clothes had blown free from the overhanging branch and landed in the water near him.

Will cursed to himself as he made his way over to retrieve it. As his hand reached and grabbed the cloth, a battering ram of strength smashed into his back, knocking him hard under the surface of the water. The massive river python had hit its distracted prey square on, and Will blacked out for a second before coming to. Will opened his eyes under the water enough to see the black and white coils of the great snake wrapping around him. His vision went red and he felt the oxygen leaving his lungs all too quickly. He thrashed and hit at the snake but his blows were useless against the king of the river.

Will was no longer in the river. Around him stood the rising sides of a great desert coliseum. Tall flag poles lifted pendants into the wind along the top balustrade, fluttering over the spectators, who were dressed in robes of black, deep blue, pure white, or the chosen color of their tribes. Will stood in the middle of the coliseum floor, dressed all in black, with a black wrap shielding his head and mouth from view. He could hear his breathing as he faced his opponent, a huge desert viper. Will held a long pole in his left hand as his only defense against the monstrous creature. He could hear his own breath loud and slow as he appraised the mottled sandy colored scales of his opponent this day. He looked into the crowd and saw to his mother and father in the stands. Their faces were mournful and as he looked on, a cadre of armored guards raised them to their feet and escorted them out of the stadium.

Will felt the flames light behind his eyes as he turned to silently face his opponent. His breathing was deep and slow, echoing to him beneath his head wrap. Will turned his gaze to the coliseum floor at his feet and slammed the end of his staff into the ground. The serpent hissed in return and from the distance of the high stands a bell rang out.

Will charged the snake. Running at full speed as the giant viper coiled back, Will closed the distance quickly. As the snake struck, Will drove the end of the staff into the ground and vaulted into the air. The serpent could not adjust in time and struck nothing but the staff as Will flew past. In the next instant, Will threw a length of rope from beneath the robes of his left arm. Fastened with two hanging weights, the rope whipped forth and wrapped around the neck of the snake. Will caught the returning end of the rope, arresting his forward momentum and slamming him into the body of the snake. He slipped the rope around itself and pulled tight. The snake hit the ground and thrashed as Will held close to its back. As the serpent moved, Will grabbed the staff from the ground and slid it through the rope's knot. As Will turned the staff, the desert viper found its air supply choked off and as Will finished the final rotation, the world went black for the snake.

Will rose from the snake, pulling his staff with him and stood to face the stands. He raised the staff over his head in victory and pointed menacingly to the faceless master of the coliseum.

The vision ended and Will felt his head raise above the water of the river for long enough to spew the water from his mouth and take a quick breath before the river python pulled him back under. Will felt the anger from the desert coliseum course through him. In that moment, Will knew that if he wanted to live life on his own terms, he was going to have to fight for it.

As he opened his eyes underwater again he saw the head of the river python inches from his own. Will's body was wrapped in coils but his hands were both free. He plunged his thumbs into the python's eyes and felt fluids pop as arm muscles honed in the forge and on the rock wall drove the thumb tips inward. The python thrashed wildly but did not give up its grip. Will took a cue from the vision of the coliseum and wrapped the sash, which was still in his hand, around the throat of the serpent and pulled tight with all of his remaining strength. The python dragged Will to the sandy bottom of the river, but then broke free as it released his body. Will put his feet into the sand and ran up onto the riverbank, doubled over and gasping for breath. He collapsed on the sand closer to the tree line and tried to recover as he watched for signs of the snake returning.

Will felt the surge of battle slowly wear off with no further sign of the python, and his breathing finally returned to normal. Naked as he had been in the water, Will went to retrieve his clothes, including the sash, which had washed up on the sand.

Still wet, and more than a little mad, Will made his way up the river bank and back to the warlock. He felt strongly like giving Malik a piece of his mind. Will was pretty sure giant river pythons were not an everyday occurrence for the members of the Fai-Kannere tribe. As he neared the mountain though, Will stopped. No, he would not mention the snake at all, he decided. If Malik had anything to do with the snake, he would be watching for Will's reaction. And even if he didn't, the warlock probably knew what had happened. After all, Will reasoned, he made it his business to never be surprised. Will took a deep breath and decided that if for no other reason than pride and dignity, he would return calm and relaxed, and not mention the snake at all.

Will passed a still slumbering Keoria and made his way into the mountain where he was met by the warlock's assistants, who led him down into a deep inner chamber of Malik's cave complex. The heat from the lava flows seemed to emanate through every wall. The walls here were black as charcoal and seemed to amplify the heat. Will was shown to a table with a long stone bench. Will guessed the pillows on the bench had been brought in just for him, as they surely would not last long in this heat. He sat down on the bench and waited for the warlock.

Shortly thereafter, Malik entered the chamber, his pale face sweating and rippling with energy. He held in his hand a wooden box, dark and lush, with a silver design inlaid in its top. Silently, he placed the box on the stone table and opened the lid. Within it was a tool of pure metal with leather wrapped around its middle. The bright polished silver metal tip seemed to undulate with waves of heat.

The warlock began an incantation and pointed his hand at the metal instrument. A shower of sparks exploded around its endpoint. Malik took a seat next to Will's exposed right arm and neck. His eyes were pure intensity as he reached for the rune-making stella and took Will's arm in his left hand.

The stinging pain from the metal tip brought Will's full attention to the moment. Malik's thick black hair was covered in perspiration and the damp heat of the room seemed to intensify as the metal etched across Will's skin. Will could hear the deep humming of the lava through the mountain, only to realize that Malik's voice had joined in chorus, a low moving chant calling forth emanations of power from the rock and molten earth beneath them. The instrument slid and jabbed, working its way across and into him. His arm switched from blazing hot to icy cold depending on the stroke and depth. As the minutes wore on, he felt himself move into a trance blessed by the rhythm of the rune maker.

Will felt his exhaustion growing as the rune neared completion and by its end he was nearly incoherent. Malik stepped back as Melthusa helped Will to his feet and brought him back through the tunnels to the guest quarters bed, where he promptly slipped into unconsciousness.

In his fever dream he saw visions, of two armored fists colliding over the Vale, of dragons tumbling out of the sky, of himself standing on an island of sand, and as he stared at it, floating in utter darkness, a sand fiend erupted out of the sand. Will, steady and silent, paused as a nameless executioner brought a sword down and parted his head from his body, and as his blood flowed, the sand fiend bore down to consume his head, his body, and his blood. The sand fiend disappeared and the scene was quiet until a few minutes later as Will's body and head, reunited, effortlessly emerged up and out of the sand. He floated up and away to see the runemaker's stella inscribing designs in gold on the inky blackness before him and he slipped back into unconsciousness.

Will awoke later that afternoon, dazed and groggy. Looking down at his arm, his mouth gaped in amazement. Malik had given him a rune and then some. A swirling interlocking pattern of strong strokes wove through the surface of the scar. Purely black, yet they seemed to emanate color, and embrace and surround a series of runes running down the shoulder and culminating in a large rune directly in the middle of his right shoulder. Will rose and made his way out to Keoria. As he began to show her the rune, Melthusa approached the two of them.

"I bring a word of good luck and farewell from the warlock," she said. "He has other business to attend to and left a short while ago. He thanks you for making the journey and hopes the runes serve you well. Keoria, he believes your rune will also serve you well and says it is his honor to work on a dragon for the first time. I believe your time here is done. We wish you safe travels."

Will turned towards Keoria and noticed that she now had a rune inscribed where her neck met her chest. He turned back to Melthusa.

"Thank you, Melthusa. I knew Malik would not take payment for the rune, but as a thank you for the hospitality that you and the people of the Fei-Kannere have shown us, please take these."

Will reached into the saddle bag at Keoria's side and produced a set of three gems, each expertly carved to show off their bluish-red coloring. Gifts from the sand fiend were now gifts to the people of the Earth Fire.

Melthusa accepted the gifts and bowed. Will gave a quick bow in turn and slipped on his riding gear and leather armor. As he and Keoria prepared to take to the late afternoon sky, he turned to Melthusa.

"Know that a friend of dragons is a friend of mine. If you ever need help, I am here," he said.

With that, Keoria flexed her wings and lifted off into the air, growing higher and higher as the purple and yellow hues of sunset began to paint the sky.

ROUNDABOUT PROTECTION
A COVEN OF THE BOWLER STORY

by Yvette Keller

Grey stopped, reaching into the cart, and I spotted another movement. A figure approaching from Carpinteria Street. Blood double-timed through my veins. No interruptions for eight generations...why me?

I'd kept watch over Grey Wolf for three uneventful hours of shuffling, chanting, pushing a shopping cart around... and around...and around...in a traffic circle pool of light. Now someone in an oversized sweatshirt appeared out of the darkness, hood pulled low. The scenario that popped into my head was bad: Grey's disguise was too good. Easy blood. The intruder would be a gang initiate assuming nobody would miss a crazy homeless person. Grey's "ritual" costume amused me, but maybe what he considered an innocuous disguise had introduced run-of-the-mill street danger to our casting.

Assuming the intruder was a criminal, he had to know he wouldn't get much from a bum. Grey's weathered suit had been black once, or maybe smoke. Under the street lights, it looked pale, the color of driftwood. It made him easier to see in 3 a.m. darkness, so I was all for it...unless it made him a mark.

Grey had just finished a circumnavigation and declared it in a clear voice to no one in particular. He was at 497, grabbing the last full plastic bag. In case an insomniac pedestrian happened to walk by, the cart bulged as if filled with the necessities of a transient life. Grey used a rumpled sleeping bag to hide the arcane ingredients. I preferred my trench coat with custom pockets but it was his turn this year.

Eyes on the slow-moving figure, I wondered: Had the old-fashioned bowler hat attracted attention? It seemed precarious on Grey's head—a facade. The hat would stay put, just like mine. Unlike mine, Grey had enhanced his hat. Stringy grey hair fell limply from the brim. The fake hair impaired his vision less than his concentration. I knew from 2012 when I'd drawn the short straw, that the casting required hyper-focus. Grey couldn't see outside his circle. He would be oblivious to the figure approaching, and even if he could see, he couldn't stop and do anything about it. That was my job.

I watched long enough to take a grounding breath. I shifted my weight, pulling out my cell. The intruder was probably just in the wrong place at the wrong time, but man, the time was really wrong. Poor dude. I wasn't sure the operation was threatened, but a criminal stereotype was heading toward my wizard. Theft made no sense, and if the guy considered Grey disposable thanks to his disguise, he was so completely wrong.

He didn't know about the skittering evils able to prey on human emotion. Sketches from the coven's book of shadows hadn't given him nightmares for weeks. That was me, unable to get a good night's sleep for most of August, after studying up on how to treat necrotic wounds left by septic ghouls...just in case.

I knew our coastal town wouldn't miss Grey specifically if someone made him a trophy kill. But the whole world was sure gonna miss the relative safety of a couple hundred years if the protections didn't get renewed tonight.

Grey rummaged for components. He had no idea he might be in danger. I phoned it in.

Cell to my mouth and tipping my chin down to muffle sound, I dialed and whispered, "Dispatch, we have an intrusion."

"Copy, Black Cat. What circuit?"

"497."

The dispatcher swore, "You're kidding me. Bystanders?"

"No."

"Cast storm. Wind too. Knock the intruder down, hard. We'll power you up from here. Hold him for the last three circuits. I'll anonymous tip the SBPD to look for...?"

"A dark hoodie and jeans. Ding-dong-ditching? Climbing fences?"

"Right. I'll come up with something and send them north of your location."

"Got it. Thanks."

I hung up as Grey crouched to scatter blessed quinoa, starting Circuit 498. Hoodie reacted, checking all directions for witnesses and stepping off the curb.

Standing up, I breathed in deep and fast until my ribs

creaked audibly.

I whispered a typhoon incantation and dispatch focused a couple members of the coven through me. Our combined intention sent my exhalation billowing down Milpas Street. At East Beach, air plunged into the sea. My magic sculpted rushing winds into an invisible bucket. Three of us scooped enough ocean to sink the cruise ship docked off the coast. I controlled my magically extended breath, forcing watery air into a curve, turning back toward the roundabout.

My lungs reversed, now empty and aching, becoming a vacuum. My jaws ached from keeping my mouth open, sucking breath back in to conjure a brutal northward squall. Inhaling a mini El Niño that targeted the intruder, I checked Grey's progress in my peripheral vision.

Halfway around the traffic circle, sorcerous power and the sudden weather made Grey increase his pace. Disciplined, trusting the coven to guard him, Grey's lips constantly whispered the protection renewal spell. No nasty goblins, ghosts—or worse—would be sneaking in via our portal. Circuit 500 would protect us for another year.

The wind wracked tall palm trees, street signs vibrated, and Grey hunched further over the handle, threading his fingers through the cart's grating. His suit flapped wildly. The weak edge of the typhoon caught him but his bowler never moved.

The intruder wasn't so lucky. Breaking waves of wind smashed him to the ground, and his hood slipped. A black emptiness and demonic violet eyes turned an execration on me. My eyes opened as wide as my mouth and I struggled to sustain the casting.

Not a criminal. Not even human. It lifted soggy arms

toward me and my breath—my spell—caught in my throat. The air around me turned thick with palpable loathing and I choked, unable to continue inhaling. The fiend had closed my windpipe from 100 feet away, which wasn't possible. I was losing a magical battle to an unnamed paranormal horror. I'd studied. And if I'd never seen it in the book of shadows, that meant it didn't exist. No ancestor had ever seen it.

Without air, the night started to fade. Sparkling bursts encroached on the edges of my vision. The air and water raised by the spell started to lose momentum, increasing my panic. I was about to black out when the linked coven members sensed my predicament. My bowler began to vibrate and a white rush of new energy surged down through my hat. Blinding, immense power filled my body, reopened my throat, and intensified my spell.

Eleven times the normal magic current rushed from my scalp to trachea. My poor brain, caught in between, ached from occult concussion. I struggled to channel the overwhelming force, burning my sinuses and sizzling my eyeballs until all I saw was green afterimage blindness.

Worried that somehow it hadn't been enough, that Grey might still be in danger, I squeezed my eyes closed, blinking hard to fade the iridescent glow. Sight returned just in time for me to watch the monster go rolling by like a twig in a flash flood. Thankfully, whatever it was, it was corporeal enough to be swept away, past the stoplight at Quinientos.

I released my breath and the magic. Staring up the street, red and blue lights approached the intersection. Dispatch's anonymous tip was wrong: the suspicious hooded figure wouldn't be caught. It would hide, or dematerialize if it could.

My phone vibrated with a text:
Nice work, Black Cat. Brace for Circuit 500.

I ducked back behind my car for protection against a geyser of light and a second blinding. I couldn't see Grey Wolf, but it was over, I didn't need to. Instead, I let my head fall back against the door, enjoying the spellbinding amber fireworks. Familiar glowing pinpoints rose silently in a column toward the moon. Falling outward, the net covered the roundabout and sank into the concrete. The protection had been renewed, and Grey's conjuring was complete.

A cart rattle and three thumps meant that Grey had jumped the fence, landing on the driveway near his tossed bags. Heaving myself onto rubbery muscles I rasped, "Let's get out of here."

Grey threw bags over his shoulder into the backseat, "Another year, another portal sealing. What was with the wet magicking, Cat?"

"Intruder," came harshly from my seared throat. I turned my Prius onto the 101. Away from police lights and violet demon eyes. After a swig from the water bottle in the car's console, I croaked out, "We're not safe."

"Not safe from what?"

"Whatever I just saw. Something not in the book of shadows. A darkness with purple eyes. It saw me." Chilled in my soul, I kept swallowing hard and wincing from the pain.

"You took care of it? That's impressive."

"The coven had to boost my power."

"How many?"

"Everyone but you."

"The whole coven?!"

I nodded. Speaking was painful and there wasn't much

to say. The car wobbled a little, my shaking body transmitting shock and fear through the steering wheel. I had practiced my whole life to keep our community safe and it had only barely been enough. What the hell were we going to do?

Grey put a hand on my shoulder, warm and solid. "Loosen up on the wheel, Cat. You saved my life. Saved the town. We'll figure it out. We turned back the ghouls in 1792, and whatever this new threat is, we'll fight until we're safe."

I wanted to believe Grey, but even as I relaxed clenching fingers, my eyes kept flicking to the rear view mirror. Any moment I might see those violet eyes looking back at me with otherworldly hatred. *Not safe,* I thought, pushing my bowler down to protect a little more of my exposed neck. That was real. *Never safe again.*

Reprinted with permission. First published in the Salt Lake Society Pagan Literary Journal, *Enheduanna,* Vol 1. October 31, 2016.

THE WEATHER ON MARS

by Nate Streeper

Emma didn't need this crap first thing in the morning. The holographic caption floated over her intended webpage, brazenly proclaiming she could EARN A DEGREE IN MINUTES!

She flicked the advertisement to the right, but it looped around her net projector like one of Saturn's rings and settled in the same obnoxious spot. She flicked it to the left, but it circled around with a vengeance and landed there, again.

Emma slumped forward on her stool. She adjusted the itchy elastic band on her favorite polka dot underwear and yawned, head still fuzzy from a night's deep sleep. All she wanted to do was check the weather at Lake Burroughs. If it was nice enough, she'd hop on the Martian Rail and ask her friends to meet her there.

She looked at her puffy easy chair where she'd laid out

long pants and short shorts. If she decided to go, what should she wear?

Crap.

Sometimes the only way to clear an ad was to double-tap and see what it had to say for itself. Emma sighed. She might as well get it over with. She looked back at the caption, pursed her lips, and tapped it twice.

The ad imploded, and for a split-second she glimpsed the weather page beneath it. But before she could spot the forecast in Burroughs, the ad bounced back and blossomed into a thousand floating words that filled her room like a star-strewn lexicon.

She slapped her hand on her forehead and held it there. What a friggin' mess. Now she'd have to eliminate each group of words independently to make the whole thing go away.

She pinched ANTHROPOLOGY, and it disappeared. She pinched EUROPEAN HISTORY. She pinched STARSHIP ENGINEERING, SOLAR SYSTEM COLONIZATION, TERRAFORMING…. This was going to take forever. Some of the subjects were floating clear over by her closet. She may as well reboot the entire net projector. But just as she decided to punch the power button, one of the floating subjects managed to catch her eye: MARTIAN METEOROLOGY (POST-TERRAFORM).

Emma paused. Martian Meteorology. Really? That one may actually prove useful.

She squinted and bit her finger. Her friend Octavia had brain-burned a load of fashion into her head last week. She hadn't suffered any ill side effects, in spite of the e-tabloid stories of cranial hemorrhaging and cognitive fallout—well, no side effects, save that Octavia now obsessed over shoes and handbags even more than she used to.

Annoying, yes. Hemorrhaging, no.

It was only ninety credits....

Emma stopped chewing her finger and used it to double-tap MARTIAN METEOROLOGY. The thousand words floating about her room collapsed, then collated into a legitimate-looking InfoDumpHoloBoard.

DONNIVAN'S CYBERSCHOOL OF INSTA-LEARNING. PLEASE TRANSFER 90CR. PLACE PADS ON TEMPLES. DOUBLE-TAP TO LEARN SKILL SET. GRADUATE IN MINUTES!

"Here goes nothing." She transferred her funds, put on the net-pads, and double-tapped.

Her mind went white and quiet. "This isn't so ba— Ack!"

Emma's head jerked involuntarily as her brain broke into a colorful flurry of activity. She felt every synapse, every neuron, every charged particle funneling data into her mind. Concepts would momentarily swirl into focus, but the lesson was moving so fast, too fast.

A few minutes later, the download stopped as suddenly as it started. A high-pitched whine slowly faded into the backdrop as her head cleared. She was sweating and breathing heavily, but seemed otherwise okay. She plucked the pads off and massaged her temples.

An obligatory diploma spit out of her printer.

Emma stood up. The weather page displaying Lake Burroughs was finally visible on her net projector. She ignored it and walked over to her room's window. She looked outside and cocked her head as she grasped wind currents, humidity patterns, and cloud formations she'd never noticed before. Her gaze wandered in the direction of Lake Burroughs, where she scrutinized the red planet's distant horizon.

She put on her shorts and headed for the Martian Rail. Pants were overkill.

THREE SIMPLE RULES

by Nate Streeper

Mother's cold hands flattened into spatulas as she tucked my blanket in.

"My Adam," she cooed. "Snug as a bug." Her rainbow mouth expanded and contracted as she talked, her red eye faded to pink. I remember feeling safe. Warm. Loved.

Every night, the same routine. And the rules. Always, the rules.

"Remember to—"

"To take my vitamins, avoid strangers, and go to bed early," I said. "I know, Mother."

"Such a smart boy." She unfurled her hands and brushed through my hair, lightly massaging my scalp with rubber fingertips.

"Is Sister almost done?" I asked. I'd had dozens of

sisters. Each one, a failure; each one, fed to the hills.

"Perhaps," she said. "We are still learning. We are still learning from the rats. But Sister will be done, someday. Now, get some sleep. Good night, my darling."

The lights shut off. She trod slowly into the room's darkest corner, her eye so pale and dim and comforting, watching, watching, watching. The room's white noise helped mask the sounds—the beating and the scraping on the outer walls, the jiggling of the rusty door valve—but it was her presence that allowed me to fall asleep.

Mother always made me repeat the rules at night, just to make sure I remembered them. But in truth, I learned best by breaking them.

I'd get angry, sometimes. It was the way I felt when I hugged Mother, the way her metal frame cut into my chest. I wished she were made of pillows. I wished she were made of me. So one morning, I rebelled. I didn't take my vitamins.

The boils manifested on my arms, my legs, my stomach. I scratched them, and they tore. My body felt like a sponge soaked in blood. Mother was so angry. She had to give me extra vitamins. I lay in bed for weeks.

Breaking the second rule was not my fault. Not entirely.

The strangers normally milled about in the distance, in the hills—grunting, twisting, flailing. They rarely approached the base of our valley until the sun began to fall. I never knew why. Mother let me play in the sand and wild weeds not far beyond our door, but I was not to go beyond the line of black and twisted trees.

A stranger had wandered to the trees, earlier than most. I was curious.

Upon smelling me, she sprinted. A scream of sorts tangled in her lungs. I could just make out her body—much like mine, but smashed and boney. She had two mouths, and one of them would not close, her tongue dripping and dangling beyond her jaw as she approached.

I think she was a sister.

I turned and ran towards the house. Mother called me from the porch, her mouth bright and loud and desperate. I slid through the door just before she slammed it, could barely hear the stranger smacking into its concrete outer surface. I tightened our door's valve until my hands were orange and shredded.

The strangers come down at night in droves. After that, I stopped rebelling. I always go to bed early. The third rule, I've never broken.

BEHOLD, I GIVE YOU THE POWER

by Ted Chiles

I didn't want to open my eyes. Throbbing temples, dry mouth, and weak limbs all spoke of tequila. The sheets were ironed and smelled of lavender so I wasn't at home. But I wasn't going to open my eyes until some fragment of last night rose up and apprised me of my current circumstances.

"I can tell you're awake...."

"Please don't yell."

"William, I told you not to play nine ball for tequila shots," she said.

The mattress shifted, and I felt her lips on my ear. Her kiss raised goosebumps.

"I got you a Coke and a couple of aspirins or do you need a Bud?"

Georgia? Georgia who tends bar at the County Line?

"Come on Professor, I got a place I need to be," Georgia said.

Thankfully the shades were drawn. Wrapped in a red kimono covered with intertwined gold serpents, Georgia looked down at me. Her hair still damp from the shower and her breath fresh with the fragrance of Crest. I was naked and sticky.

"Hi," I said and reached for my vapor pen.

"You can't smoke in here."

"What time is it?"

"It's 9:17, and you have twenty-three minutes to get showered and dressed. Your clothes are in the dryer," she said, handed me the Coke, and popped two aspirins in my mouth.

"Where's my car?"

"Back at the County Line. Now get in the shower." She started to pull the covers off the bed. I held on and she laughed. "Come on Professor. I saw every inch of you last night and kissed a fair portion of it too." She looked at her watch. "You got twenty minutes. I'll make you an egg sandwich. You can eat it on the way."

Georgia turned her black Ford F-150 into a crowded gravel parking lot in front of a single-story red brick building. A white cross was painted on the wall to the left of the door. A small sign that read Red Rock Holiness Church was posted on the door.

"Why are we here?"

"My Uncle Mike is preaching today. I'm not missing him for you."

With my best professorial stare, I radiated disapproval and disappointment.

"You can wait out here or walk back to the County Line or come to the service," she said, exiting her truck. "Want me to roll down the windows?"

The next twenty minutes were spent leaning against Georgia's truck, vaping and analyzing the cultural implications of the assembled vehicles. Most were domestic. Red was a popular color, which could be attributed to either political or sport affiliation, and I wondered what color they would have chosen if the Crimson Tide had been the Blue Wave.

The faint sound of voices and a keyboard could be heard, and I discerned or imagined a few Amens. The volume rose as a guitar joined the keyboard.

"What the hell," I told the empty parking lot and opened the door.

Later, I would remember the tall man strumming an old SG, which seemed out of place. He should have been playing a Telecaster or a Gretsch Country Gentleman, not the Gibson guitar Pete Townsend played and smashed in the early days of The Who. The woman at the Casio keyboard fit my idea of a rural church organist with her long hair and denim dress. The oak cross above the makeshift altar was finished in a high-gloss varnish similar to the tables at Cracker Barrel. The congregation looked country. An expression I never heard up north, yet often bandied about in the small town where my college was located. But none of this I consciously saw as I opened that door.

What I saw was Georgia in a light-blue dress with small white and red flowers. Don't ask me what kind. I've never been good at botany or biology or herpetology. But I know a fucking rattlesnake when I see one, and she was holding a three-foot rattler in her hands and dancing with eyes closed in what can only be called rapture. I froze, unable to speak or move. The need to urinate spread across my crotch.

A man, Uncle Mike I assumed, pulled a thicker, longer snake from a wooden box. This snake had a pattern of diamonds down the back. He turned and offered it to the congregation. No one came forward. Uncle Mike held the snake high above him.

Georgia swayed with the snake. A convulsion shook her, and her eyes, her blue green eyes, opened and she looked at me. My fear was flushed and replaced with the need to be back in the drunken dark. Away from harsh florescent lights and the pulsating music. Safe from these serpents but with the knowledge of what she had held and how she held it in pure belief.

Georgia slowed and moved toward me. The congregation's gaze followed her until she stood with her arms outstretched, offering the snake.

Standing there, I wanted to be the child I once was, safe in my room. The window cracked open to let the night air in. Shielded by my prayer, *If I die before I wake, I pray the Lord my soul to take.* But did I have a soul to take? And who would want such a soul?

"Take him William," Georgia said. "HE will protect you."

The guitarist stopped playing and the organ died out. The congregation quieted. Uncle Mike stood behind Georgia, his snake back in the box. My hands turned palm up and my arms began to float, then the rattler turned its cruel eyes on me. Its forked tongue came and went. I heard a hiss and ran out the door through the parking lot down the road toward the safety of my books and my classroom. I ran as long as my smoke-compromised lungs would allow.

When I slowed to a walk, panting, drenched by sweat, surrounded by the dense green landscape, I looked back hoping to see her Ford F-150. No truck appeared. No tires on the road could be heard, only the sounds of insects and the beating of my empty heart.

THE RIFT

by Nicholas Deitch

I won't pretend to understand all of this, but I know what I know. I know that this life—these bodies and the terra firma of this sensible reality—is not at all what it appears to be. There is more, my friend. There is much, much more.

I have been beyond the edges of the firma. You have, too—though you are probably unaware.

There is a place, between wakefulness and sleep, that we all pass through on the way to our dreams. But this place is not of sleep, nor is it of the visible world. Rather, it is a plane, a shift, a realm within time, or perhaps outside of time— remember, I, too, am only trying to understand—where consciousness escapes the limits of the physical and familiar. I call this place *the rift*, and I have wandered there, near every night, almost since my memories began.

I've never shared this with anyone, but something

happened that nearly pushed me to my brink, and I can no longer keep it hidden. I feel the need to tell someone. Anyone. Indeed, I must, to free myself of the doubt that churns within me.

This is my confession.

A night like any other. I undressed and brushed my teeth. I turned out the light and slipped between the sheets. As always, I quieted myself. Conscious of my breathing, the shapes and shadows of the room begin to dissolve. I let the darkness enfold me in its tide, let it lift me, out and beyond.

And I am free, of breath, of body.

I move through the door—yes, *through* the door—of my small apartment, along the hall, past other doors beyond which other lives are lived. The walls shimmer, the furniture fades. I look about and I can see the vestiges of inhabitants, present and past, or yet to come—a woman getting dressed. A boy, hiding from his sister, a dog barking, a man at a table weeping—or is he laughing?

There is joy, a baby in the arms of a new mother. A couple on a couch making love. Workmen setting beams, fitting windows, forming concrete. All of these spirits, or perhaps mere traces, like fingerprints, that linger where time is of no consequence. The building dissolves, as do others nearby, and the streets and the lights, the land laid bare, wild and verdant, rolling grass and trees adrift beneath an auburn sky, a time long before—or perhaps long after—this time I call the present. I can roam here, moving back and forth within the shifts. I can voyage out beyond the stars, or below the sea. I can stay, in perfect solitude, not a thought or care or...

Or so I think.

Leland.

I strain to hear, or to feel, for the source of this intrusion. Someone calls my name.

Leland.

I opened my eyes, sunlight streaming through the curtains. My head was full of dream stuff, some conversation with my mother, long passed, and then walking with Natalie, or maybe she was hiding.

Natalie? Was she with me? Of course not, for I knew full well that she lay in a bed, in a room, in a house, connected to a machine, locked in perpetual sleep. The memory tore at me, the mechanical keeper of her prison ceaselessly whispering in her ear—*thhhhhp, thhhhhp, thhhhhp.*

Guilt washed over me. I had not been to see her for some months. This, after weeks of vigil, sitting by her side, holding her hand, wiping her brow, avoiding eye contact with her mother, trying not to trip over Sheba, her toy poodle, yipping to be held or curled up on the floor in her little bed in the corner of the room.

"It wasn't your fault, Leland." But Dorthea's eyes belied her doubt. The bastard nearly hit two other cars, after he hit mine. She tidied the room while I sat by Natalie's bed, the one-sided conversation now so familiar. *Thhhhhp, thhhhhp, thhhhhp.* "I just don't understand what you two were doing there at that ungodly hour."

What was I supposed to say? I was fucking your daughter, Mrs. Jameson, and she was fucking me. And she's an amazing lover—did you know? And she's lying here beside me, while you blather on about something neither of us can change.

What was I supposed to say?

Days and weeks, I stayed by Natalie's side—before work, after work, into the night, through the weekends. Holding her hand, reading to her, some of her favorite poetry. And yes, I caressed her breasts, and kissed her lips, still full and warm. Dorthea almost caught me with my hand in her gown. I wanted so badly to give my Natalie some bit of pleasure, but I'm no Prince Charming. I'm just a guy who loved a girl, before some shit-head fucked it all up, and sent my car careening over the edge of Highland Drive, sending my dear Natalie into a purgatory of perpetual sleep.

Thhhhhp, thhhhhp, thhhhhp.

I never saw him coming—the bastard was still out there, free as you please.

Months passed. I just stopped going. What was the point? My touch meant nothing. My words meant nothing. Dorthea always with her doubting looks, guarding her daughter's long lost virginity, the goddammed sleep machine with its ceaseless chiding, the little dog waiting hopefully for her mistress to rise. Natalie, the sleeping beauty of my charming impotence.

And then this intrusion, a voice that called to me through the shifts.

Leland.

Unheard of. Never in my twenty-six years.
Natalie? Is it you?

I stood on the sidewalk in front of the little house. The small porch, so familiar. If I thought about it hard enough, surely Natalie would open the door to greet me, sandwich plate in hand, little Sheba prancing about her feet, and we could sit again on those steps, sharing bites, laughing, licking mayonnaise from each other's lips, the amazing taste of a full wet kiss baptized by tuna fish and a can of Pepsi.

I walked up to the door and raised my hand, two quick raps. A moment passed and the curtain drew back. Mr. Jameson's face, dim through the dirty glass. The curtain fell into place. The door opened.

"Didn't expect to see you coming 'round anymore." He looked much older, dry and empty, still wearing pajamas. "My wife is out."

"I just wanted to see how Natalie was doing." I offered lamely.

"Same as always." He opened the door and turned back toward his easy chair, a game playing on the T.V. "You know the way."

The room dark, the curtains drawn against the bright sunlight, Natalie lay exactly as I'd left her. That beautiful face, her cheeks flush, her lips full, eyebrows of dark chestnut, hair slightly lighter, with the sheen of a recent shampoo. And her neck, so lovely, with skin the color of cream, dusted by the most delicate freckles, that damned trach tube intruding through a hole that shouldn't be there.

Thhhhhp, thhhhhp, thhhhhp.

I sat down. She looked like she could open her eyes and sit up at any moment.

Thhhhhp, thhhhhp, thhhhhp.

I pulled my chair close, little Sheba pawing at my shins, starved for the affection her mistress used to shower on her. I scratched behind her ears and stroked her fur, surprised at the peace this brought me. Sheba curled into my lap and went to sleep. I reached out to take Natalie's hand. Warm, familiar. I brought her fingers to my lips and kissed them. Her skin smelled antiseptic, not the lovely musk that I remembered and longed to taste again.

Oh, Natalie, where are you, baby? Please come back.

I sat there, holding her hand to my cheek, my head against a small pillow, Sheba nuzzled in my lap. I quieted myself, and let the darkness come.

Thhhhhp, thhhhhp, thhhhhp.

I slip through the rising tide. The room shimmers, the bed glowing softly.

Baby? Nat?

Leland, please.

Nat, where are you?

I need you, Leland. I'm so alone. I don't know where I am. The porch? But everything is different. I'm afraid.

To say that I am astonished is a lie. I'm terrified. I have caused this, I have lost her, to wander within the rift, within the purgatory of a sleepless dream. I move through the shimmer, through the walls, past the old man there in his easy chair, sucking on his beer, watching the game, watching his life disintegrate, unaware of the vestiges that surround him—a woman sweeping, a child with a toy, a dog licking himself—previous occupants, future occupants, their presence in the rift unaffected by time.

Leland, please.

I move through the curtained window to the porch. Natalie is here, on the steps, her beauty a strange translucence. Beyond the porch, the land is wild and windswept, shifting near constant.

She is with me.

Leland, what happened? What am I doing here?

Should I tell her the truth? Do I even know, myself?

Natalie, there was an accident, some guy in a truck. We went over the edge. You were thrown from the car.

Yes. Yes, the truck. My father. I saw his face. So angry, so hurt.

What are you talking about?

Leland, I need to go on. Please set me free.

Natalie, what are you saying? What's this about your father?

Leland, please, just set me free.

"Who let you in?"

I sat up with a jolt, little Sheba startled from my lap, tumbling to the floor. Dorthea stood in the doorway, with her hands on her hips.

"You have no place here, Leland. Natalie is getting along just fine without you."

Thhhhhp, thhhhhp, thhhhhp.

"I needed to see her, to tell her I miss her."

"Well, she doesn't miss you, I'm sorry to say. And neither do we."

I stood to leave. "Fine. Whatever."

She looked away, wiping the dresser with a dust cloth. I walked down the hall, in all its glorious normalcy, and into the living room. Mr. Jameson still in his chair, snoring, his pajamas twisted, an empty can of beer in his lap.

Natalie's words came flooding in. *The truck, my father, I saw his face.*

"What the hell did you do, old man?" I kicked his chair.

He snorted. "Wha? Who?" He scratched his belly and looked up, squinting.

"You followed us. That night. You tried to kill your own daughter."

Astonishment in his eyes. Then anger. "Get the hell out of my house—"

"You tried to kill us. Or maybe you just wanted to kill me."

"Keep your voice down, goddammit." He shot a glance toward the hallway.

"Maybe Dorthea should hear this—"

"No, don't!" He exhaled, his voice falling. "It wasn't my fault. I was just sitting there, with a six-pack, watching the lights—and the lovers. I just watch, is all, and—" Another glance at the hallway. "And I saw her face. My little girl, naked. I'd been watching my baby girl screwing some shit-head kid in his piece-of-shit car."

"You hit us on purpose, you old bastard."

He pushed himself up. "No! It wasn't like that. I was piss-drunk. I wanted to kick your ass and take my baby home." He was almost sobbing. "I didn't mean to hurt her, I swear—"

"What's going on here?" Dorthea stood in the hallway. "What are you talking about?"

"Ask your husband." I turned and walked out.

You need to understand, it's not like riding the rift is some kind of super power. I don't get to know all and see all, and have all the answers and save all kinds of lives and shit like that. It's more like a carnival ride, really. I never know where it's gonna take me, and most of the time I don't even know what it is I'm looking at. Hell, I didn't even know someone could talk to me—if you can call it that—until Natalie reached out for help. Twenty-six years, and I never knew.

But just like being awake, in the rift our minds can make choices—even if we aren't aware. That night I turned out the lights and lay down like I always do. But my head was raging. All I could think about was Natalie lying there alone, her body afloat on a hospital bed, her spirit lost in the chasm of the rift. And her dad. Jesus, what a mess. He's not a bad guy. He loved his little girl—I could tell by the way he looked at her, how he lit up when she walked into the room. But goddammit, he's a drunk, and he's miserable, and he was stuck in that little house with his daughter down the hall, knowing he put her there—both of them prisoners of that horrible little machine that wouldn't let her go.

Thhhhhp, thhhhhp, thhhhhp.

I closed my eyes. I tried to quiet my thoughts. So much turmoil. So much pain.

The darkness comes crashing in, the tide a whirlpool sucking me down. The rift churns and rumbles—or is it me? I am flung into the night, across the sky, the city translucent, breathing, gasping. Highland Drive, Lover's Point. The cars lined up for a drive-in movie that isn't playing. Chassis rocking, swaying, lovers mingling, sweat and steam. There, my crappy old Saturn with the torn up bucket seats in full recline. Natalie. I'm with her, and she's making ferocious love, her body bending, rolling, sliding. Ecstasy, she arches back and then collapses into my arms, her breath like nectar. We are in this moment one, eternal and unending.

I see the time. Shit. I have to get her home. We pull away, and my headlights catch a faded sign on the side of a truck, Westridge Service. Natalie gasps and crouches down.

'What's wrong, babe?'

'Nothing. Just keep driving.' And then something hits us. My car is tearing through the guardrail, tumbled over the edge. How the hell did I walk away?

I stand by Natalie's side, the room aglow in the light of the rift. The machine whispering, *thhhhhp, thhhhhp, thhhhhp.*

Leland, please.

Natalie sits up, her vestige, naked and luminous.

Leland, do something. Help me. I have to go.

What can I to do? The machine pumps away, the ceaseless chant of unwanted breath. There's a switch, and a cord, and a plug in the wall. But I'm not really here. It's the goddammed rift. I have no control. Hell, I'm lying in my bed, three miles away. What the hell can I do?

My eyes go to little Sheba. Her small spirit like a tiny nightlight, curled up on her bed in the corner. Can I reach little Sheba? I have never considered such a thing, but I have felt the spirits of those around me, the vestiges of life that inhabit this place of in-between. If Natalie can reach me....

Sheba. I feel for her presence. *Sheba, girl.* Can I meld with this little fluff ball?

Sheba...

I reach up with my leg and scratch at my ear. That's a bit weird. I stand and stretch and paw at the blanket of my mistress. I turn in a circle on my bed, looking for just the right spot, and—I stop, Sheba, and I—there in the wall is the plug, the cord hanging down, the electrical lifeline that feeds the machine. I reach up and nudge the cord with my snout. Firm and unbudging. What can I do? I bite into the cord, clamping down as hard as I can. A jolt runs through my being, an electrical shock the likes of which I have never felt before. The machine hisses, sparks and smoke bursting from the monster of breath.

Thhh—. The beast is silenced. Little Sheba lays on the floor.

Natalie trembles, and she is gone.

I opened my eyes and lay in the quiet dark. In a few hours, Dorthea would rise and go to Natalie's room to find that her daughter had passed over. But over to where? The rift is just an in between.

Natalie is gone. An act of mercy, I hope. An act of love. But from where we stand, you and I, I guess I killed the one I loved most in this whole tentative world.

THE DEMON LOVER

by M.K. Knight

Folks say he almost killed me, *the poor child*, and there's truth to that. Others point to my preference for solitude as proof of my damaged psyche, and perhaps that's true too.

Only I know the real truth.

No one ever suspected. Not one of my husbands or the children we raised, not my publisher, fans, or critics. I use a pen name, of course, and invented a trust fund to explain my wealth to those who know me as the frumpy stay-at-home mom. It takes little effort for me to hide.

My innocuous lies are never questioned, because, who really pays attention to Mom, anyway? Hours spent locked in my sunroom, remembering the touch, fingers hot and dry, scratchy caresses and kisses like flame jumping inside my mouth, melting me into a blur of agony-induced spasms. Shame creeps in to the hollow silence of the aftermath, banged out on the keyboard for another bestseller from the reclusive novelist and poet.

Silence is key to my success. It is the seal that keeps my memories intact, that allows my skin to feel him boring down into me and I am fourteen again, breathing in his sweat and the pheromones that make me crave his power over me. Breaking the silence would puncture that seal, memories escaping like air from a balloon, precious treasures lost to me forever. The bestsellers would stop, the world would wonder why, and my secret would emerge, my private shame once again a public humiliation.

I imagine he is actually with me, not just in my head, the subsequent bruises and burns a reminder that I am his, as if I could want to be anything else. He commands me, each time, to tell no one, a promise I make gladly, knowing that telling would end his dominion over me. It would leave me with only the life the world sees for me, lost in the shadows, forgotten and overlooked.

My human lovers are always a disappointment. I try to enjoy their small gifts, to keep the memory of him from destroying what little intimacy I have with them. I fail every time. They call me cold and dispassionate, eventually finding lovers of their own, while I enjoy myself in the sunroom.

Despite their ignorance, my spouses and children have a knack for using my books in family disputes. Husband #2 gives me a volume of my short stories, and suggests I could learn something from it. At fifteen, Sylvia leaves a copy of my poems on the coffee table to provoke her stepfather, my third and final husband. He tosses it in the fireplace and grounds her. I kick him out and buy Sylvia everything I've written so far. I tell her to read whatever she wants, but I never tell her I am the author.

I am eighty-two now, and my grandchildren have children of their own. Sylvia's daughter Tracy moves in with her twins and thinks I am unsafe in my sunroom. She wants to move my computer to the downstairs study and I tell her no. We argue for weeks. One Monday, she persists at the sunroom door, uninvited, until I unlock it and let her in.

Her confession tumbles out like a broken necklace I have to thread back together. She is sorry, but worried, very worried, and that's what led her to do what she did and now she is even more worried. Beside me on the wicker couch, she takes my hand and tugs at my sleeve to reveal a mosaic of purple, green, and yellow. She calls him *That Man*, although in her illicit recordings he is no more than a shadow, but he is clearly assaulting me, and I clearly need help, as the marks on my arm clearly illustrate. I hold my breath when she claims to know the big family secret no one is allowed to talk about, that she read the newspaper articles and even found the original police report on microfiche. She tells me I don't need to be a victim anymore.

When she is done talking, she stares at me, waiting for a specific response, my silence underscored by a fly in the corner window. I cough, pull my arm away from her, and recover my bruises. I am mortified by her perception of me, a frail and damaged object in need of her protection. My truth is far less humiliating.

Tracy is disturbed when I ask to see her video but shows me anyway. My elderly face is out of place with my memory of the encounter. I'm grateful Tracy sees only his shadow for he has changed, too, his once-beautiful smile now a hideous leer of jagged teeth and forked tongue, his body nothing more than maggot-colored skin wrinkled over sinew and bone. *This is my real lover.* I have a twinge of sadness for our interrupted passion, but I can't feel the sensation of his body anymore. He will never come back. I know this already.

My granddaughter misinterprets my tears. She tells me not to worry, that forensics are better these days, that I should tell her who *That Man* is so the police can arrest him.

I walk to the bookcase and find a first edition of my debut novel. I open to a favorite passage, but my once-vivid memory of writing it is stripped down to basic facts. The feeling is gone. I can no longer invoke him.

I hand the book to Tracy.

"That was no man," I tell her. "That was my muse. I doubt anyone will see him again."

TRUNK ROAD

by Tom Layou

I knew something was fucked when Petey said to bring a Saturday night special, but what was I gonna do, not get coke? Withdrawals had my cold, sweaty shirt clinging to my achy back. "You gotta throw it in the smelter or some shit," I said. "My prints can't turn up." He couldn't hide a look that said they might. I handed off the stolen pocket pistol wrapped in a dirty t-shirt and turned for the door.

Misread that, I thought, turning back to see the last couple flashes, my knees sagging. As I carried the image of Petey's face to the floor, a scar faded but the terror did not. His face flashed youth before I heard a light pop and it was whited out with whipped cream, dollops splattering the circular board that framed his face.

I was eight years old, playing games with other kids

while grown-ups by the fire shot beer-launched bottle rockets at each other. An older boy in flannel was loading the toy catapult with whipped cream for us. He held the can upright with a finger against the nozzle and placed it in his mouth, breathing deeply. He held it a second and let out a slow, vacuous, "Hah! Petey Pie Face!"

Petey stood and yelled, "Don't p-fuckin' call me Petey p-Pie Face!" dripping and spitting cream. It was the only time we ever heard him stutter but it stuck.

I watched young Petey wipe his eyes and when they opened I was looking at me, feeling that powerless little kid anger as I watched me laugh with the older boy. When he blinked again I was still looking at me, dead on the floor now.

I could feel panic squishing around me as Petey looked around the room. A florescent Bud Light sign and a Scarface poster on the wall framed with multicolored spatters of spilled and flung drinks. A large wall mirror advertising fake-ass O'Doul's. In the living room were flat pillows with heavy sweat stains and crusted blankets, all piled on a couch that looked equally found, nobody paid for anything around here but drugs.

From where Petey stood I was oil-streaked work clothes with a gut, long hair, and a trickle of blood spilling out. He began to pace, kicking an old stool and an end table that got in the way. Petey punched the mirror and stared. There were a few more wrinkles and not as many teeth as you should have at twenty-three, but Petey always fixated on the crease under his left eye. Facial reconstruction. Petey fucked up just right one time and instead of plain disappearing, he was a big enough piece of shit that the offended party could afford to leave something on his face. A reminder, and an advertisement, that he fucked up somewhere. Dealers considered Petey's sub-human status a credential.

I watched him lean down and reach in the pocket of my jeans for the coke. It was crammed in the corner of a sandwich bag that had been twisted into a long rope, torn off the rest of the sack and tied with an overhand knot. Petey untied it as he stepped into the kitchen and dumped some of the bag on a mirror. With a razor blade he teased out two enormous lines. He held a short straw to his nostril with one hand and placed the other on his forehead to keep his hair out of the way.

He sniffed the first line and I was in a white stone bell tower, deafened by peals of granite sunlight. Petey stared across at the cracked O'Doul's mirror a few seconds in pure detachment before shrugging and leaning down for the second line. His next breath put me in a mountaintop blizzard, wondering if I would topple from the crest, thrilled to find what that sensation would be.

Petey stared at the failing cocaine, motionless. I was blasting across the cosmos but all he felt was the cold and clammy of withdrawals creeping in. He put a fist through a cabinet, indifferent to glass shattering inside. "God damn it!" Petey yelled. He burst across the room and started kicking my body. "Motherfucking goddamn fucking mother fucker!"

Petey kicking the shit out of my body was like listening to a tantrum in the next room, the rage poured around my euphoric bubble of cocaine joy. When Petey tired he leaned a shoulder against the door, placing a foot on my hip. He flopped his other arm to the cell phone in his pocket.

Dialing sounded distant, but the answer was augmented and shook through my being. "Yeah." The euphoria made that easy turn to anger. Lee. Of course it was Lee.

"We're uh," Petey reached in his mind, "We're all good here."

"On my way."

Petey put the phone in his pocket and went back to the kitchen. He put his hands on either side of the mirror and stared down at his face.

Petey, you shitbird. You worthless fuckwit shitbird.

He drew out two more lines and railed them back to back. I was a toy airplane on a string, soaring magnificently around the room but Petey stayed anchored.

In the mirror across the room I watched Petey's chest heave before he stomped back to my body. He rolled the couch against the coffee table, clanking pipes, bottles, and a heaped ashtray to the floor. He snaked a blanket from underneath, laying it out next to me. My shroud.

Petey freaked when he heard feet on the porch until he recognized the knock, less a proscribed rhythm of taps and thumps, more anything that doesn't sound like the repetitive, driving slams of police at the door.

"Gimme a sec," Petey called, grabbing my ankles and pulling hard to free the entrance.

"Hurry the fuck up."

"Sorry," Petey called out. "Just a second." He tripped on my foot and said, "Sorry," again as he opened up, whispering, "He fell against the door."

Kicking the door closed behind him, Lee tugged the snowy cuffs of his leather gloves. Early forties, neat, trim, no time for a moustache. "Fuck are you doing shooting a motherfucker in the doorway anyway? What if he got out?"

"I just, fuck, man!"

"Screw it, let's roll him up in this shit." Less than a minute after arriving, Lee was ready to take the body.

"Hold on a second," Petey said. He grabbed the eight ball and straw before throwing on a windbreaker.

"You gotta be fuckin' kidding me. Can we get rid of this now?"

"I'm sorry, I'm sorry," Petey said, shaking as he lifted my feet.

"You're like a pile of shit but less useful." Lee opened the door and looked out before lifting under my arms. This corner of Muldoon belongs to the Russians, they don't give a shit about anything. It's an ideal neighborhood. Instead of a leisurely toss into Lee's truck, they had to cram me in the back of a nineties Civic, a cracked pile of rust and dents. Lee had presumably exchanged drugs with a fiend for temporary and unspecified use of their car.

It was like watching on TV, a Petey camera, as I saw him scatter trash over the blanket and slam the hatch on my ankle. Lee glared while Petey moved my foot and closed the hatch. Petey looked in every direction as he took his place in the passenger seat. Lee looked like he was leaving for groceries.

As Lee drove out of the neighborhood, Petey slumped into the trailer court turns I wasn't to know when first brought around. My head was wrapped in a blanket instead of a blindfold but I wasn't in there this time.

There was no speaking as the car shuddered onto the highway. Colder, and clammier, Petey couldn't stop tapping his toe. He started to roll his window down but changed his mind. Listening to snow in the wheel wells, he pictured a tire burrowing into miles of powder. He looked at Lee, then the floor before running his hands over his neck, thighs, the knees for a moment, then his shoulder. He watched snow fluttering to the ground in tall beams of lamplight. Wiper blades clearing large flakes that landed wet on the windshield blended with soft, clumpy sounds under the car, a serene, monotonous bubble. The controls on the heater didn't work but miraculously it was stuck on something warmish.

Petey had begun to rock, and Lee ignored the motion until he heard the *sniff*, and, "Gn-haa!"

I was a dog with its head out the window, gleeful.

"For fuck's fucking–listen, asshole," Lee said.

Petey wiped the back of his hand against his pants and kept it there, his elbow twisting forward.

"We have a goddamn dead body under old newspapers and Dorito bags, in a busted-ass car rented from a fucking dope fiend. We can get in an accident, or pulled over, and now I gotta worry you're gonna have that white, powdery, Captain Obvious angel's share smeared all the fuck over your face."

Petey snapped his hand back to his nose and pinched it, wiping what he failed to snort from the web of his hand. "I'm sorry," he said, "I railed some fat lines and nothing happened. I feel like I ain't had a bump since yesterday."

Lee said, "You do too much."

"You don't give a shit. Nobody gives a shit." Petey's voice cracked, "Just, fuck!"

"Ah, shit, Petey. Just hold off 'til we get past Eagle

River, OK? Eagle fucking River, it's right up the road."

Petey nodded, staring at his vibrating heels.

"And use the damn straw," Lee said.

Back here in headworld that left me in a hurry to get to Eagle River, and a little too much time to think. I hadn't been robbed per se. But getting lazy on a Fairbanks run and shipping blow north instead of driving out, no matter how careful I'd been, was going to get me in a lot more shit than getting burned in person. I also couldn't explain *careful* meant taking my teenage cousin with her undocumented fingerprints to the porn shop and spending five hours figuring out how many grams we could stuff in a gutted vibrator or seal up and jam in a bottle of lube.

It was hard remembering, though, when I could feel Petey fiending as he watched long ridges of snow on the highway. Petey remembered driving a plow truck for Lee as a kid. Using a pickup fitted with a scoop he'd plow snow into a long, low bank to carry off swipe by swipe to an expanding pile. Petey would pretend he was driving a giant nose as the bank narrowed with every pass, gasping when the plow slammed into the pile, lifting the truck's back end. The last scoop was the best, that most authentic solitary line disappearing between plow edges, headlight beams illuminating shadowed tufts of snow tantalizing as enormous cocaine lines. One last slam into the pile, then, "Whoo!" a sprinkling of white fluff dotted the hood, and off to the next lot.

Petey imagined the nose until the last Eagle River exit shone through the blizzard, opening the highway to precarious nothing.

Fucking finally.

Petey unzipped the inside pocket of his coat in guilty silence. Some powder floated onto his shirt from the open bag. He put the straw inside and took his time-out pressed in the corner between the passenger seat and door. Petey took a deep sniff.

I was a beacon of incandescence locking the car to the black underside of the clouds. Petey waited a second and started to stamp his feet, slapping his knees.

"Petey," Lee said, "I'm going to need you to calm down."

Petey turned his head side to side twice and leaned into the window, squishing against it. Under the luminescent column of my being, I could feel Petey's sadness. In his best times, it had been a low mental hum.

Deep snow jostled the car occasionally, gentle sprays thrumming the underside as the heater whirred. We passed the exit for the disued Old Glenn Highway. In the snow, this car wouldn't make it to Jim Creek. At least I escaped the northern cliché of disappearing into the Wal-Mart of south central Alaskan body disposal.

"Listen," Lee said, "I appreciate you telling me about Jeanie and that piece of shit back there."

I'm the piece of shit. Ben, for the record.

Petey sat forward again, a little hunched. "Yeah, I mean, you know, I had a hard time with that and all. I mean, I wouldn't want to, uh, rat anyone out any way, but, I just thought about, well, how mad you'd be, and I," Petey sniffed, "I just knew it was, I had to tell you. Ya know?"

"I do," Lee said with an icy benevolence, "and I appreciate that, I really do."

"I'm glad, you know. 'Cause, even though it was something you needed to know, I was kinda," Petey touched a hand to his forehead and then pinched his mouth, "kinda worried after I talked to you like that you'd, I didn't want you to start, to have questions about me, ya know?" He pressed his arms to his side and I could feel him wishing he had another coat.

"I don't have any questions. I know you're no slouch. You've had a rough couple years, your parole officer always dicking with you, some serious hits, and that'll fuck with a guy. But I know you're solid. You got no worries with me, bud." Lee paused in vicious silence. "Motherfucker. Thinkin' I didn't know about that bullshit with Jeanie."

OK, so there was also that time I made out with Lee's daughter behind a bar.

The car jostled and whirred. Lee said, "Then the fuck-monger lets some asshole rob him. All right, it happens. He should have been watching his shit better. Then he comes douchin' around, wants us to front a ball before he's paid up, fuck his ass. Don't ever think you did the wrong thing, Petey, because Ben was a selfish jackfuck dickbag."

What can I say? He had me pegged.

While Lee talked, Petey slowly folded himself back into the corner, exhausted. The car jolted right as it bit fresh snow leaving the highway, but Petey didn't notice the scraping underneath. Lee feathered the accelerator as the back end carved "S" turns in the snow. Lee mumbling, "Come on, come on" filtered thinly into Petey's skull, blending with the heater's steady whir.

"You OK over there, buddy?"

Petey flinched awake. "Th-yeah, I'm good." It burst out as one word. Then, slowly, "I'm good."

"This fuckin' thing," Lee said, shaking his head as he killed the ignition. "Guess it got us there. A beater with a heater, right?"

Petey tried to sound cheerful, "Yeah, ya got that right."

"Let's go in." Lee opened his door and stood.

Petey froze halfway out of the car. "This is my cabin."

Lee became flat. "Yes, it is."

Petey looked around the property, his grandfather's cabin, tucked small in the woods and rotting where it touched the earth. Around one side of the cabin was a wood pile. Behind the pile a blue tarp covering some outdoor hardware stuck out chest high. "What's up with that tarp?"

"I don't know, Petey."

"Think I should check it out." A vague lilt couldn't decide if it was a question.

"Let's go inside first and bust a line. I think you could use it."

By all means. We haven't done a line in ages.

Petey entertained a protest, then lowered his head and walked toward the unpainted cabin door. Snow sprinkled over the tops of his shoes but not enough. Petey said, "Who do you think plowed?"

"A good Samaritan."

The one room cabin was sparse and incomplete inside, a few pieces of plywood and seventies floral wallpaper, but mostly unfinished walls with tufts of pink insulation sticking out by the studs. A table and two chairs, faded brown surfaces on dull orange legs, waited in the center.

Lee scraped his boots across the room and pulled a black zippered fold of leather like a shaving kit out of his jacket, placing it on the table. He sat and unzipped the kit, removing a small mirror. Petey tried to sit before his apprehension showed. He was getting tired. Petey watched as Lee pulled from the kit a razor blade, a metal straw, and a small jar of cocaine with a snouted top. Pressing a lever on the jar, Lee dumped a small mound on the mirror and divided it into two slightly uneven lines. Petey's every muscle was locked with tension, and he felt a darkly exhilarated sweetness in his core.

"Aren't you gonna?" Petey asked.

Quit fuckin' me around, Petey, and sniff the blow.

Lee sat back in his chair. "You know how it works. I set 'em, you pick."

Petey put the straw to his nose and chose the fatter line. The fearful sweetness surged as he leaned down to meet his own eye in the mirror. He did not expect Lee to let him sit back up. He inhaled with the greatest sincerity and hope of all his being.

I skyrocketed through spiked cherry cola and beach fire sunrises, wove through fleeting joys and saw old loves without the sadness of loss, plucked a string of fruits from a miles-long curving row of cream-topped treats.

Petey leaned over the mirror a long time. When he sat up, Lee had a .45 in his lap.

"So, Petey," Lee had gone from flat to viper cold. "Ben owed you money. And you owe me that money."

"Well, yeah, Lee, but that's what I did it for, for his six g's."

"I needed that money last week. I told you that."

Petey settled an apologetic look on the floor. The room flashed, and I was splattered on the wall with his childhood memories, mist dancing in front of the hole.

God damn it, Petey, you stupid fuck.

Petey and I sat looking out a window. In the driveway, Lee flung the blue tarp onto the snow. With a gloved hand he savored the red hood of his pickup, then the bright yellow plow he'd bought for it. That morning Lee must have shoved snow into a large mound where the driveway met the woods. It did not take him long to move the pile on top of the car with my body in it. Inside, the remaining white line gleamed on its silver mirror. With each swipe of the mound Lee piled a scoop of white over me, a monument to sheer waste that wouldn't stand five months. Falling snow would obliterate any tracks and by the time the heap melted it was going to look like Petey had some explaining he decided not to do. Lee would leave the cabin door open to smaller scavengers for meat, larger ones for a gun, and no one was going to ask any questions.

When Lee finished burying the car he got out of the truck and smoked. After he threw the butt in the snow, he dialed his phone. "Yeah, honey, just got the truck back," his voice jovial now. "Yes, it is the perfect weather. Yeah, I got to try the plow out a little, sweetest anniversary present I ever bought me."

While they bantered I felt the last line fade and turn to a frigid cosmic sweat funnel being pulled from me. I watched from the splattered wall as Lee clomped snow into the cabin and sat across from Petey. After a blank minute, he lifted the straw and inhaled.

On the wall, dust blew through the bullet hole and swirled to the floor.

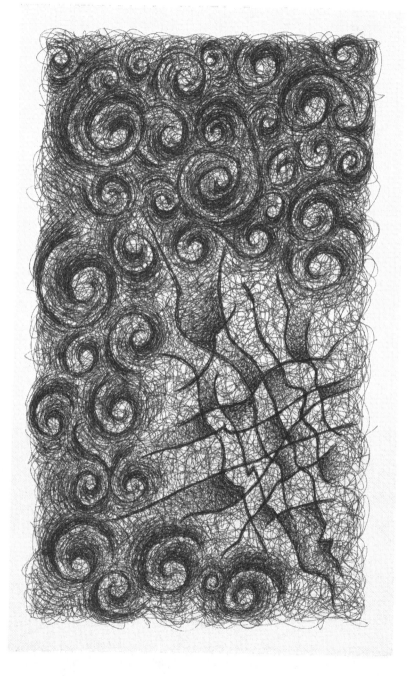

"Untitled June 22, 2016" by Stephen T. Vessels

POEMS

SERPENTINE

LETTER FROM THE GUEST EDITOR OF POETRY

by Sharon Venezio

Our journey into the heart of the serpent begins with the assertion "Everything I know I learned from snakes." In the opening poem, "Luminary," snakes have wings, bring wisdom, and green the garden. As we follow the serpent, it becomes our mother, the ghosts of our ancestors, the mouth biting down on the singing body of the cricket.

As these poems came together as a collection and began to speak to one another, I noticed a growing tension between all the representations of a snake. Each poem talking back to the other, defying the other, expanding the other. We are both snake and garden, mother and daughter, carrying both venom and cure, punishment and redemption.

Best,
Sharon Venezio
Guest Editor of Poetry

LUMINARY

by Terry Wolverton

…like Nuah, the goddess, riding
out her self-generated waters.
She got her name changed to Noah.
From "Into Eternity," Eloise Klein Healy

Everything I know I learned from snakes. They wound around my hips, glided up my arms, whispered secrets into the shell of my ear. A winged snake showed me herbs to bring its dead mate back to life. Plants began to speak to me. Leaves would hiss and roots would twist and flowers dripped nectar venom.

They showed me the veil between living and dead is porous, and I began to call back those who had traversed its weave. I called because I missed them, because the world without them was pale and sad. I summoned and they came, resumed breath and music-making. They had opinions and wanted everything to remain as it had been.

The living weren't grateful. They'd cleaned out closets, spent the inheritance, occupied the family home. The living rely on the dead to make room for them. And the Underworld was depopulating like a Rust Belt town. The mayor was mad; he demanded his tax-base be restored. Said I had to be stopped.

So Grandpa killed me with a thunderbolt. Because he could. He tried to make it seem less cold by spinning me off into the firmament, sculpting my body from stars. My form entwined with snake, head in one hand, tail in the other. In stories they told later, they'd say I was a man. Of course. They called me Ophiuchus. Called me purveyor of poison, trafficker of malice.

But no, I am a woman who talks to snakes, invites their wisdom. A woman with a snake is a dangerous thing. Before men took over, snakes had wings, were rainbow goddesses. In Africa, they call me, Mami Wata, "truth of the waters," my waist wreathed in snakes. In Egyptian Arabic, I am called Hawaa, another name for Eve.

MOMMY AS SNAKE I

by Nina Clements

The living mother
is a snake in the garden,
waiting to strike. The apple
is filled with poison,
and she wants you
to taste it.
She cannot bring
herself to bite you
directly, but she would urge
you to take the knife
to your own flesh.
This is how she loves you.

THE WISDOM

by Yvonne M. Estrada

Grandmothers always have
a little sadness.
They sing the old songs
that cut deep into the soul.

Ghosts of the ancestors appear
in the form of snakes;
this way they can shed
their stories.

Grandmother sings the old songs,
hard-core gangsters cry
like newly widowed women,
no one is ashamed of tears like these.

MOMMY AS SNAKE II

by Nina Clements

She chooses to live as a snake
in the flower garden, the orchard.
There she is, lurking behind a decorative
rock. There she is, waiting for the flesh
of your bare foot. She wants you to step
on her, to earn the venom in the sting.
We are all afraid of her bite
and trod with care in the grass.
But she hides and hides inside us,
coiling in our hearts.
She made us; she can destroy us.

STILL LIFE

by Lisa Cheby

After Christina's World *by Andrew Wyeth*

The hardness of the earth impresses itself into Christina's right hand as it holds the brunt of her weight. Her left hand reaches away towards the house, the lone grey resident watching over the field. The blond grass caresses her wrists and ankles, reminds her that all flesh is her flesh. Her nipple-pink dress: the only sign of life here. Though she seems perfectly still, she stokes a fire as thigh heaves against thigh with each breath, like the pulse of roots drawing up earth's fertility. Her feet stretch to new beginnings as her heart yearns home. She is paralyzed. In the middle of the field under an overcast sky belying the warm breeze lifting Christina's brown hair, one day to be grey as the barn, home to field mice and last year's hay.

BACK TO THE GARDEN

by Yvonne M. Estrada

When the primary source cannot be found
it is said to be hidden or occult

Early stages of stars hidden in dense clouds
can only be seen in infrared light

It can be treated with radiation
most likely there will be memory loss

Copious amounts of radiation
are emitted by massive forming stars

Cells multiply in distant locations
like in the brain, often forming masses

Young budding stars may form by coalescence
of two or more protostars of low mass

Red giants die fast, white dwarves live longest
I know a song that says we are stardust

LATE SEPTEMBER

by Kim Dower

7:11p.m., dark again
as daylight, reluctant felon
turns itself in

We tread water at dusk
ask the moon to forgive us

remember when
we were about to begin

& Spring broke out in a sweat
all of us on the steps
late evening sunsets
now a memory
as we ease into
the starched white pillow
of winter

This hurts my back,
my father would say
late July days at the beach
when he'd reach beneath the kelp
scoop us kids out of the ocean

We didn't care
about our father's pain
our mother's boredom

just wanted more
of the same—staying up late

party cake, loving the sun
for telling the moon to get lost
as we'd be tossed

by the waves
runaways, ice-cream and sand
crusted between our hungry fingers

YOGA FOR THE TOO MUCH ALONE

by Lisa Cheby

I hold a pose out of alignment
so the teacher will adjust   a shoulder / hand / foot /

when we all play corpse
I remain   fully aware   waiting

for her to press my shoulders   root me to the earth
then a fingertip to the third eye,
                   an evangelist willing the blind:

See, you are real.

THE SINGING BODY

by Sharon Venezio

As the Santa Anas whip past the eaves of your sleep
and rustle your dreams, I lie awake, listen to your breathing.

The night sounds like a broken animal, like the crickets
you fed to your pet snake. I turned away

before it was over, before the corn snake seized
the singing body with its mouth and pressed down.

You laughed, said it's just nature. My body turns
beneath the sheets, craving the heaviness of water,

to be water, to know what drifts out returns again,
to be immeasurable.

THE SCARECROW BRIDE

by Terry Wolverton

Rain scatters light across the valley, no bonfire
to burn down the night. Wind sweeps the harvest moon from
the city, where her groom invents the lost hours. He
snatches songs of crows from the cold sky, assembles
scraps into ceremony, wants to satisfy
her cravings. She's home, piecing together the red
confetti of her days, arranging a picture
of her dreams. Mud stains stripe the mattress. She wants to
be intact but cannot forget she is made of
straw and leaves. Stirring cream into the river, she
sugars her lips with vows in a language he
cannot speak. They will spend lifetimes discovering
how touch goes wrong, but for the moment, he awaits
her in his shiny jacket, waits to gather the
flood of her green veil in his devouring fingers.

MEDUSA

by Chella Courington

Athena saved me.

It happened so suddenly.
Strands slipped away, piled at my feet
enough to weave a shawl.

But then something strolled along my scalp
like curls tousling in the wind, pausing
to check their way. Tongues flicked
to smell my skin.

Now, at night, their heads curl
near my face. They stroke
my head, absorb
my warmth, press
against my skin.

When a twig snaps or a leaf crunches, they hiss
sensing intrusion. Usually a male who fancies
he'll be the one to take me like Poseidon.
Tearing my clothes, fouling my body
with slimy hands, forcing me under him.

Divine males are no different
from mortal males.

Their scales are black.
Once the color of my hair.
Her curse, my blessing.

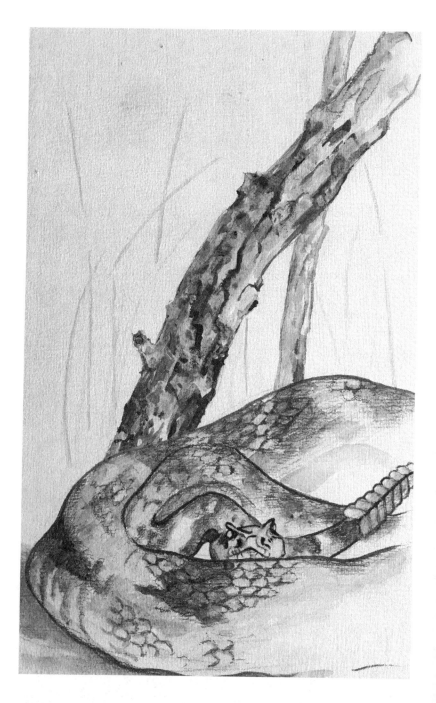

"Sam's Friend" by Robin Gowen

THE
YOUNG

PESHMERGA

by Gwen Dandridge

2004 Erbil, Iraq
2nd Battalion 327 Infantry

"Help me understand. Why is a fourteen-year-old Kurdish girl being sent by herself to live in America?" The captain steepled her fingers and waited.

An electric fan whapped around and around, barely stirring the hot, dry air. I dug my cracked thumbnail into the flesh of my palm as I stared beyond her desk. To her left, a gold flag, with a white-headed eagle in its center, caught my attention. Screaming Eagles, 101st Airborne Division.

Mawoma, my mother's father, snapped his finger across my wrist to get my attention, an impatient gesture from an impatient man.

Though I couldn't raise my eyes above the captain's bars

on her fatigues, I repeated what I'd been saying for the past hour, "Half-Kurdish. My father is with your military, Stephan Dupres. He came with the Americans after the Kuwait war."

I could feel Mawoma's gaze hit me. Yes, I'd avoided her question, but nothing could make me say the words for why I was being sent away.

The captain spoke again, repeating the list of papers needed, the rules that must be followed, and the difficulties in emigrating during a war.

I ran her words through my head before translating them to Mawoma with a brief, "She says it will take time."

Mawoma slapped the bundle of papers against the steel table with his vein-lined hand. "Tell her this is what we have, Nazê, all you need."

The gold charms on my hat brushed across my forehead as I turned to him. "I did." He could understand as well as I.

"Tell her again."

The captain's buffed fingernails lay like stone chips on the other side of the grey desk.

"Mawoma says that these are the correct papers."

She pursed her lips, flipping through the documents again. "Nace, I see that, but as I keep telling you, this isn't something that happens in a day or a month. It takes time. No matter the paperwork."

I corrected her. "Nah-Zey." The Americans never said it right.

There was a flicker of annoyance in her eyes. I lowered my head so she wouldn't see the anger and distress in mine.

"Fine, Nah-Zey." She leaned back. "Where is your mother?"

"Dead." Saying the word brought up a bleakness that threatened to swallow me. I pressed on, not stopping to breathe. "She was an interpreter for you Americans during the Kuwait war."

She pointed to my grandfather, a crease settling between her eyes. "You have relatives here—kinsmen."

I hid my trembling hands within the folds of my dress. I remembered the last time I had seen my aunt...my grandmother...my uncle. Remembered the wailing as they were buried under the hard rocks beneath a clear blue sky.

Remembered why I was here.

Mawoma snapped my wrist again. "Lift your head, Nazê. Let the part of you that is Kurdish speak."

I clasped my hands together so she wouldn't see them trembling. "The PKU and KDP dispute. The fighting came to us—even in the mountains. My aunt was *Peshmerga*, one of the freedom fighters." I had trouble speaking the next words. "She died—and many others also."

Her eyes softened and the crease fluttered away. "Yes, we heard. Such a shame. One of many atrocities, I'm afraid."

She wrote something down, then shifted the papers on her desk. "Your father was with Operation Provide Comfort?" A crease settled between her eyes. "That division has been gone for years."

I shrugged, unwilling to let her see me react. Yes, he was gone, gone for years. "Maybe," I whispered. "Is that what the papers say?" Beside me, Mawoma straightened in his chair as if unwilling to bend to its contours. "We...I need to find him. My my mother wished that I be reunited with him."

"When did she die?"

The white walls tightened around me. "Two years ago."

"...And your most recent correspondence with your father?"

"Three, almost four years since I saw him last." My thumbnail bit further into my palm.

Her eyebrows raised. "So why now?"

At another snap upon my wrist, I gathered the lie I had been told to repeat. "My grandfather has chosen to honor my mother's wish that I be reunited with my..." I stuttered the next words. "...my American father."

The captain stirred across from me. "Yes, I heard you the first time. Let me check and see if they've found your name on the list of emigrant requests. What did you say the spelling of your father's surname was? D-U-P-R-E-S? I may have seen something about that name. Wait here, please."

She walked around her desk and left through the door.

Mawoma shifted in his seat and stood, only the slightest tremor betrayed his weakness. "This is for the best, Nazê. Fallujah is under siege. You'll be safe in America. *Inshallah.* Your rifle and knife will go to your cousin. Our fight continues." The effort of speaking triggered an unsuppressed hack from his throat. Little specks of blood landed on the clean linoleum floor.

"Your rifle and knife will go to your cousin. Our fight continues."

He pushed the chair back and shuffled to the door. I knew what was coming, what he had made clear before walking into this building. He was abandoning me forever, like a cracked and broken pot, no longer useful. I shook with the effort of not throwing myself at his feet, promising I would never awaken the village with my nightmares, never threaten my cousin again, never cower with every shift of the wind—never be who I was now.

"All will be well. *As-salamu alayk.*" *Peace be upon you.* The door clicked as it closed.

I was alone.

The eagle on the flag seemed to watch me hook my feet around the chair legs. Otherwise, I might float away in despair.

In the distance, a door slammed. A phone rang over and over, but no one answered it. Within minutes, my world filled with noise. The sounds of military voices as they peeled me off the vinyl seat.

I knew if I moved I would no longer be me. There would be nothing left, not my kinsmen, nor my mother, my aunts…not my land, not even my dogs.

I couldn't speak. My eyes saw nothing but the tattered, blood-flecked handkerchief after Mawoma coughed.

Their voices continued, but I had nothing to say. I no longer existed. The girl I had been disappeared, slowly evaporating into the air where I sat. The shell that remained of me couldn't move.

My memory failed me soon after, my mind a maze of fear and loss.

The next thing I remember was the slam of refugee camp gates as they locked behind me.

My mind and body reunited, and I flung myself at the

fence, clawing to get out, begging. Behind me voices rose and fell, hands pulled at me. I fought, pressing tightly against the barrier, the metal biting so deeply the crosshatching stamped into my forehead and my cheek. If I stretched my head up and looked beyond the grey buildings and black cars, in the far distance I could see the rolling line of my mountains. Nothing could move me, not away from the wire wall, away from my mountains, my land. The moon rose, and still I clung there, my fingers interlaced in the wire, my mouth dry from crying, my throat raw.

Each day more sounds outside. Jets screaming above, trucks rumbling, horns blaring, the wind howling across this flat land leaving nothing but dust. Within the compound, other sounds filled my being. Ones I wished to never hear again: babies screaming, children wailing in pain, angry men scrabbling over food, and women mourning lives lost.

The third day I stopped my tears. I was a freedom fighter, a *Peshmerga*—those who face death—a Kurd. We were indomitable. Nothing could break us, not the loss of kin, not this refugee camp, not the fear. By day I watched, strong, silent, hoping that Mawoma would reconsider and return for me.

But when night fell, I relived the sounds of guns shooting, bombs dropping, and helicopters approaching. My screams came as my nightmares descended. Strangers cuffed me, clamped my mouth shut. I couldn't escape their pain, my pain. Which was it? I hardened myself. I ate sparingly, looked for ways to escape, and kept to myself.

Locked within this mountain-less plain of white tents and lost people, I was the most lost of all.

CLEAN-UP ON AISLE THREE

by Jordan O'Halloran

My mom told me she found out about me at a truck stop bathroom. She hadn't had her period in over two months and found herself craving nothing but gummy worms and stale tortilla chips. She was sixteen.

My grandpa chased her out of the house the day after she peed on that stick in Arizona. My grandpa doesn't believe in God, but that day he did. He claimed that my mom had the devil enter her between those legs, and that what would be arriving those quick eight months later was sure to be the worst mistake of her life.

So, hello, nice to meet you. I am that mistake, but you can call me Lucy. Lucy Love McBride is my full name, but my friends call me LL. I was born and raised here in the desert, but always pray for the rain.

My mom and I live with Chuck, her boyfriend.

She says my SS (sperm supplier) moved to Michigan right after I was born. There's a few pictures of him somewhere in the attic in an old shoe box, but they are getting pretty faded now. It kinda sucks knowing that I will never know my "dad," but Chuck is all right. He always wears the same old gray and green flannel on his days off, has toothpaste stuck in his messy beard at all times, and fills the fridge with half-full drunken beers that he swears he's going to finish. If having six or more beer cans in the fridge with a few sips taken out was an Olympic event, Chuck would win every time.

Chuck has one redeeming quality, though. He gave me a job at the grocery store Smile's he inherited from his filthy rich dad, Raymond, who died last year. The cops found him dead on Aisle Three with the fresh fruit. The blood ruined all of the apples, and the Fuji and Red Delicious had to be thrown away. Everyone claimed his dad was killed by Chuck's stepmom, Veronica (perfect evil name, right?), but it was actually a murder by Chuck's brother James. The police found a person wearing a Barack Obama mask, shooting Raymond from behind on the security cameras, and the gun with James's fingerprints on it a few days later.

Don't get me wrong, I do feel bad for the guy. But it's not like he was a saint or anything. He always claimed that I was a "bastard child," and that Chuck was an idiot for choosing to be with my mom, or as he so fondly called her, Trainwreck. Besides, Raymond wouldn't even let homeless people use the bathroom in the store. He cheated on Veronica all the time with the produce manager at Smile's,

Lucinda. Everyone knew about it the entire time it was happening. It was usually hush hush, but they made it way too obvious to hide. Anyway, back to work. More later.

When Raymond died a year ago, the clean-up on Aisle Three wasn't just him; I turned into a total mess. My counselor at school told me that talking to someone who wasn't Ben, my boyfriend, would probably help me feel better. The thing is, I feel alright most days. My therapist Dr. Prince diagnosed me as bipolar and told me I have a lot of signs of PTSD. I have visions at times of the blood dripping, turning the aisle bright red. Maybe it was because I was there the morning he was found. Chuck and I drove over to Smile's together, which was our normal routine at the time. He let me drive his black Dodge Ram, Batman. He washes his "baby" every weekend on his days off. He won't even let my mom use it to go get her cigarettes down the road.

Everything was normal. We had our powdered donuts that turn my fingertips white from the sugar, and our chocolate milk that usually gives me a mustache like Chuck. He unlocked the front door, turned the lights on, and I went around to the meat department where I work to get dressed in my apron that's constantly full of gross animal smell. As I laced up the back, I hear the loudest yell of my life.

"LUCY! CALL THE POLICE, RIGHT NOW!"

"Why, what's going on?"

"No time for questions, just call them."

I grabbed my cell phone out of the front pocket, and

with my shaky hands somehow called, 9-1-1. I didn't know what to say, just told them to come to Smile's Market on the corner of 7th and Camden as soon as possible. I hung up and walked out of my bubble of the meat department, and saw a long trail of red. I also heard lots and lots of crying, followed by "Why?" and "What the fuck, Dad?" Chuck was a mess, and the only thing I could think of initially was to give him a hug. That's what I would've wanted.

The worst part was seeing his dad just lying there. Smile's isn't really the place anyone in their right mind would choose to die. His face somehow looked so surprised with two huge bullet holes in his chest. I wasn't feeling good by any means. The fluorescent lights burned my eyes, and everything swirled into one. The walls started closing in on me. My chest was closing. I couldn't breathe. I just wanted Ben or my mom to come and save me. But Ben wasn't answering, and my mom was probably hungover. She was at the bar the night before.

Detective Mick Kane and his crew were there within five minutes. The howling of the police cars made the hair stand up on my arms.

"Hey, Monkey, what does MILF mean?"

Monkey is my mom's nickname for me. She has been calling me that for as long as I can remember.

"Mother I would like to fuck...why?"

"Oh, just some really cute guys at Smile's today called me that when I went in there to get some cigarettes. I think they said they went to your school."

"Oh, they seem like great people. I am definitely going to go introduce myself to them as soon as I go barf in the bathroom."

"Lucy, don't be such a drama queen. Not everyone can say they have a mom that's super hot. I like this word MILF. I can see it in lights now, Kelly McBride, MILF of the year!"

"You are so weird and embarrassing. Why is your skirt so short? I can see your underwear."

She looks at me as if it was the most obvious thing in the world, drawn-in eyebrows down and everything. "That's the whole point, baby girl. Your MILF momma is broke, and wants to get some free drinks tonight. I deserve it. See ya later, sweetie! There's a pizza in the freezer for you. Tell Chuck I am at my art class."

Ugh. She is so annoying, but she's all I got. She tells Chuck she is doing art therapy to deal with the "tragedy of losing Raymond." Being a seventeen-year-old with a thirty-three-year-old mom is super irritating and really sucks. My mom is always craving validation and attention. The stupid thing is that she always tends to get it, but from the wrong type of people. Before we met Chuck at Smile's, we had gone through an amusement park of crazy people. There was Tim the clown who wasn't even funny and always seemed to smell like rotten cheese, and Tina when my Mom was in her "man-hating phase." She wore a lot of black that year.

My favorite guy of all the losers before Chuck was this dude named Erik. He was the one that introduced me to what being vegan is, and was the best cook. My mom and I used to go to animal rights rallies with him, and one time after one of those rallies, my mom took us to KFC. He saw us there when he was walking by, and broke up with her right away in the restaurant, and we never saw him again. Why she chose to go to the one right by his house still baffles me.

The creepy guys lurking everywhere around this town are always saying things like, "Oh, is that your sister?" or "How many years apart are you girls?" I am always wanting to kick that smug, toothless smile off their unwashed, dirty faces. My mom is a magnet for those idiots. It literally happens to us everywhere we go: even at the gas station or when I pick her up from the bar when she has had too much vodka.

It also doesn't help that she dresses younger than I do. For my birthday last year, my Aunt Michelle got me a gift card to Forever 21. I don't even shop there, but my mom sure does. She came back the next day with the ugliest leopard heels I have ever seen in my life. She is supposed to be a Size 9 but always buys a Size 7 since they make her feet look smaller. In the leopard heels though, her heel was sticking out the whole time. It was hilarious but only to me. The blisters on her feet shut her up for a while.

She also dyes her hair bleach blonde every week. I am not talking about natural dirty blonde, think more Marilyn Monroe walking through a snow blizzard. She spends about $5 a box and it usually ends up looking pretty good the first few days she has it in her roots. My Mom is a brunette, but you would never know by looking at her. She also spends about three hours a day putting on makeup. No joke.

She always tells me that I helped her grow up, and to never make the same mistakes she did. I can't help but feeling she means I was her mistake. I don't ever want children though. Ben knows this and he agrees, too. The idea of a human sitting in my stomach for nine months and eating all my food is the most unappealing thing in the world. If anyone is going to eat all my food and take up my entire free time, I'd want it to be Ben or Snowball the neighborhood stray cat who's pregnant again. For the fourth time in two years.

❖ ❖ ❖

Still at work; on my lunch break. My mom keeps calling me to remind me to pick up some steak for Chuck's birthday tomorrow. We have this dumb tradition where everyone at Smile's Market comes over to our house for employee birthdays. We all have cake and pretend to like each other. Ever since Raymond died last year, we have more team building now. Before the dude kicked the bucket, it was great here. You would get to take the day off and no one would care or question it. Now, the store closes on the first Saturday of the month to celebrate all the people's birthdays that fall on that month. We always eat the same red velvet cake with the grossest cream cheese frosting that my mom makes. Everybody brings their entire families, which usually include babies. I hate babies. I think they look like potatoes, and they always seem to smell really bad.

Most of the people who come to the parties are doing it for Chuck. With Raymond gone, a lot of them feel bad for him. Raymond was the only family he really had after his mom left them, and his brother killed Raymond. Pretty sad stuff, but it's still annoying them taking my deserved Saturday away from me. I fake my smile enough for people to have a good time, but go to my room immediately after the last guest leaves. I hate it, but at least Ben will be there. Ben is my boyfriend and we both work in the meat department together. I like to call it Hell and it's on the end of Aisle Five, you can't miss it.

Hell is usually where I spend most of my free time when I am not studying for school or birdwatching. I am always complaining about the smell. I haven't eaten meat in three years. Chuck knows this, but him and my mom like to punish me for what they call my "bad attitude." That "bad attitude" is honestly 95% of the time caused by them, though.

I stole the car once to go rescue Snowball the cat that was trapped in a fence behind Ben's house. There are kids at my school who are doing drugs, getting tattoos, and brag about getting alcohol poisoning. But me leaving at 2 a.m. to go rescue Snowball, I am the worst teenager in all of Arizona.

I have since promised my mom, I will start being good though. Chuck is turning forty, his Dad's death day is coming up, and people are constantly quitting or asking for more money.

Julio, Lucinda's son, is here. He is asking where he can get a paint job for his car. Apparently, he is wanting purple flames and aliens in spaceships all over it. Ben knows a few people who I will let him know about. I am constantly surrounded by idiots; when will it end?

❖ ❖ ❖

Honest question here. When do people stop having theme parties? I want to say ten or eleven, right? Don't get me wrong, the Avengers and Moana are pretty cool party ideas if you have a little kid. If I had a kid and they invited all their friends over, I would definitely have a theme. But my mom thought it would be a great idea to buy a bunch of Spider-Man decorations for Chuck's party. He is turning forty, not seven.

Ben and I are in the kitchen, blowing up balloons that she got at the Dollar Store. I told my mom she should wear this red wig she bought for her Lucille Ball costume a few years back to be Mary Jane, but she didn't get it. For those of you who don't: Mary Jane Watson is Spider-Man's girlfriend.

The smell of burnt cake fills the kitchen. My mom hung up the piñata under our own willow tree that I named Fred when I was four. All the snacks are done, and all the ice in the cooler with the drinks is melting fast. With Chuck turning forty this year, my mom is hoping to have healthier snacks. His doctor told him to stop eating so much meat. He is even starting to take heart medication so he doesn't end up like that guy from the *Sopranos*.

"What do you think, Luce?"

"About what?"

"My outfit, of course."

"Mom, its Chuck's birthday. I don't think people are going to care what you are wearing."

"Can't I just wear heels with spider webs and get one positive comment from my daughter? Is that too much to ask?"

She slams the back door, cigarettes and neon pink iPhone in hand.

Ben looks at me, "What crawled up her ass?"

"I'll find out."

I walk in the smoke-filled, humid garage. She is scrolling through Facebook, and her contoured face is lit up by the bright screen of her phone.

"Mom, what's going on? Are you okay?"

"Yea, hun. Everything's great."

"Cut the shit. It's me you are talking to, not Oprah on her talk show."

I notice her hair is parted on the left side of her face. She never does that and her eyeshadow is so heavy she looks like a raccoon.

"I just don't know anymore, Luce. Chuck hit me last night, he gave me a black eye. He keeps saying it's going to stop, but it doesn't. I know the stuff with Raymond still hurts him, but that guy was the worst, you know that. Don't tell Ben. I want this to be our secret."

"Okay. What can I do?"

"Nothing. I am going to get us out of this shit hole, though. We can all go to Seattle like you want. My treat, baby girl."

Never in my life has my mom been this honest with me. Who would've thought something so terrible would unite us for that split second? I am hoping everyone gets here soon, so the party can just be over already. Oh, wait. I hear the truck of Lucinda's alcoholic boyfriend vibrating outside.

Breathe in.

Breathe out.
Let the phony smiles and awkward smiles begin.

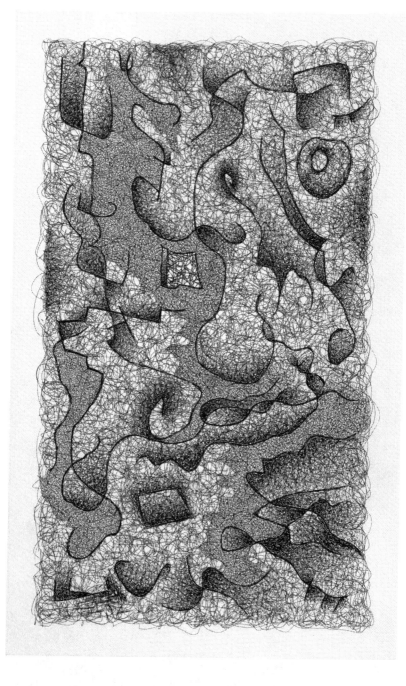

"Untitled December 30, 2015" by Stephen T. Vessels

LYRICS

SONGS OF HOPE
AND CHANGE

LETTER FROM THE MISTRESS OF SONG

by Laura Hemenway

My role as "Mistress of Song" continues to evolve, and I've been learning how to be a discriminating curator of song lyrics.

It isn't important to me, when selecting lyrics, whether a writer is in a particular age group, or what famous person they've studied with, or whether they have a significant Facebook following, or how many recordings they have to their credit.

My criteria for selection, this time around, in Volume 2? Well, I guess it's kind of like putting together the most wonderful dinner party. It's alchemical, in a way. All of these writers light up a room when they enter it, with their sheer presence. All of them have fantastic creative musical projects that they are leading. All of them have a unique sound and style of composing. And if we had a concert with the five of them, it would levitate the audience to a new level of positivity and enlightenment!

Songs are mysterious. Everyone experiences them differently. All I can do is share my favorite writers with you, the readers, and hope that they will spark something in you, and change your life for the better.

Which brings me to the theme: Songs of Hope and Change. Two words that have been part of my meditation practice for most of 2018.

Bertrand Russell once pointed out that maintaining a sense of hope can be hard work. In the closing pages of his autobiography, with its account of his many activist years, he wrote, "To preserve hope in our world makes calls upon our intelligence and our energy. In those who despair, it is frequently the energy that is lacking."

Margaret Mead wrote, "Never doubt that a small group of thoughtful, committed, citizens can change the world. Indeed, it is the only thing that ever has."

Introducing Annika Fehling, Ian McCartor, Cathryn Beeks, Donna Lynn Caskey, and Gabrielle Louise. I encourage you to seek out the melodies and voices that intertwine with their lyrics. And look for upcoming performances and events related to these artists at SBLitJo.com.

Best,
Laura Hemenway
Mistress of Song

BEAUTY QUEEN

by Donna Lynn Caskey

You were raised by strong, smart women
Who were agonized by the size of their thighs
Who cursed dark circles under their eyes
And any mark upon their skin
They reminisce about when they were thin
Then you grew up to look just like them

You were teased and tried to be tough
When you were just a geeky teen
Reading grocery checkstand magazines
Lose more weight to be enough
Look like a model to win their love
You never thought you measured up

Well, I declare, you're complete
With flaws that make you dear to me
Darlin', you're my beauty queen
Darlin', you're my beauty queen

Misprints make the most valuable stamps
Losing our balance is just part of the dance

Well, I declare, you're complete
With flaws that make you dear to me
Darlin', you're my beauty queen
Darlin', you're my beauty queen

THE LOVE STILL SHOWS

by Donna Lynn Caskey

Red geraniums planted with care
Crooked bangs since mom cut our hair
Pink-trimmed dress all washed up and pressed
Unaware just how much I was blessed
No one meant to be cruel
They sent their baby off to school
Photos taken so long ago
My folks are gone, the love still shows
My folks are gone, the love still grows

A stranger's smile eased my despair
The friend who called out of nowhere
My heart touched by a hopeful song
The way you held me until the dawn
Such little things have seen me through
Such little things can be so huge
More than we may ever know
The moments pass, the love still shows
The moments pass, the love still grows

TIMBUKTU

by Ian McCartor

Well I got these wheels turning,
ain't no gear 'sides go,
I want to move I want to know
A far fever, burning boy it stings,
I got a fire and got me wings

Hear my tale,
love to tell you more,
I'd love to trade you one for yours
One day I'm cleaving kiss goodbye,
yeah free my mind and break the ties

I got this feeling and
I don't know about you
But I'll fall to pieces
If I don't find my way to Timbuktu

I can't stay hidden locked behind these walls,
can't close my ears to kill the call
My hands holding blood and sweat and tears,
it's adding up over all the years

A bell ringing like a whistle blow,
oh Lord I pray and Lord I know
Can't stay dammit,

do before I die,
to share the laughs and share the cries

I got this feeling and
I don't know about you
But I'll fall to pieces
If I don't find my way to Timbuktu

EYES TO SEE THE WIND

by Ian McCartor

I was born to this world with our vision, decisions
The journey of life calling me out

Learned how to dream with the mission's revisions
My failures and friends teaching me how

When I just couldn't get through a surface to serve us
A wall that was holding me off

I was touched on the hand that was nervous, assures us
And told me to start singing this song

I have eyes to see the wind
Visible to everyone who lifts their heavy heads
I have eyes to see the wind
Given to me to see the end

Well, a young man made plans in a good world,
the wood curled
From carving and claiming my start

But spending my money on white pearls for nice girls
Wasn't healing the holes in my heart

Now to see what will last past the burn, oh infernos
Is something I'm longing to know

A friend brought to mind the words of eternal
And now I know just where to go

I have eyes to see the wind
Visible to everyone who lifts their heavy heads
I have eyes to see the wind
Given to me to see the end

AUGUST

by Cathryn Beeks

Sunday evening when it's quiet everyone settles in.
It's been a hot week, another hard week starts over again.
In the factories in the workshops in the tunnels in them mines,
get yourself out of the sun, find someplace to hide.

They tell stories of the days
when people would play,
swimming in the ocean
right out in the open.
Now we must hide inside,
only last as long as our water supply.
August may end us.

It's been a decade, maybe more, since the rain filled our cups.
All the food and most the people have long since dried up.
Still a few of us hanging on but it won't be long,
the only thing that will be left is this sad, lonely song.

ONLY LOVE

by Cathryn Beeks

Romeo and Juliet are sitting in a corner,
this is going to end bad someone ought to warn her.
Look at that, look at them, don't let it make you jealous.
Love ain't no story someone else tells us.

Love is for the patient ones
who know just what they want
and never settle just because
time is running out.

Love is like a tidal wave sucking in the ocean.
Stronger than the most powerful of potions,
it'll make you crazy, love will drive you mad.
It'll make you think this is the best you ever had.

Love cannot be denied,
traded or rejected.
Everything that is alive
eventually is affected.

Every single one of us has had some experience
with love or lust or something more serious.
Even people we don't know will end up in the game,
the ultimate equalizer, it keeps us all the same.

Love is for the lucky ones
who find their true intended
when they take a wrong turn
and get into a fender bender.

Love is going to scream your name
Love is going to rock you.
You will never be the same
only love can stop you.

STRANGE SUMMER SNOW

by Gabrielle Louise

When I die won't you carry me up the canyons of stone
where the light echoes like the prettiest song—
and cast out my ashes, a strange summer snow
spinning down on the current that'll carry me home.

And if you can't find me: look under your boot-soles.
Pick up a fistful and be at peace.

I'll water the almond tree, its roots are my own—
mirror the branches, where sweet blossoms grow.
Come and gather the petals, in the pale moon they glow,
Shaking down on the green grass
like a strange summer snow.

And if you can't find me: look under your boot-soles.
Pick up a fistful and be at peace.

In a basket they're carried with wicker and wine
to give to a lover on her wedding night.
Oh, they're tossed like confetti, a new baby cries and moans
while everyone's barefoot and dancing
in a strange summer snow.

MADE FOR SOMETHING MORE

by Gabrielle Louise & Justin Thompson

Oh, there's freedom in this country
You're free to pace the floor
and if you don't think the room's locked
try the door

There's a young man down in county
he was stealing for his family
first he was unfettered, now unfurled
Oh, a man can own a gun
maybe he can rob someone
But a man can own a bank and rob the world
Oh, you can make it in this country
unless you're gay or sick or poor
Yeah, if you don't think the room's locked
try the door

They put the poor kids in the back room
thirty-six a classroom
And the second day of school there's even more
They're damned if they're not reading
They'd be better off just cheating
'cause all that really matters is the score
We teach 'em freedom in this country
then we send 'em off to war
And if you don't think the room's locked

try the door

No more blank stares
or blinking eyes
Don't turn away, don't deny
it's time
to recognize

I was just a child when it happened
He shut me in the bathroom
Asked me which way I would prefer
So I grew up half-thinking
I was put here just to please men:
to smile, laugh...defer.
But the woman in me came to know
I was made for something more
Oh, if you don't think the room's locked
try the door

Oh, every woman in this country
has been shaken to the core
So I say if the room's locked...
storm the doors.

(For our inspiring first lady, Michelle Obama, and for
my sister Sarah Isobel, who teaches our children love
and equality, and for whom I always want to make the
world a better place.)

Made for Something More / Louise & Thompson

GREENLAND

by Annika Fehling

Oh, this light
Like a pounding heart
No escape
It tears apart

Open up
To the crystal sharp
Endless sky
It tears apart

You and I
Whitefire, water
You burn me down
I put you out

Wild and wide
The sea, the dark
Death and life
It tears apart

You and I
Whitefire, water
You burn me down
I put you out

WEST OF SKY

by Annika Fehling

West of Sky
East of stars
You've come a long way
To my heart
Many centuries have fallen and passed
Many lifetimes gone
Still you found
Your way back at last

West of Sky
East of stars
Like a candle
Flickering in the dark
Sometimes when I reach out
It's easy to find
Other times I stumble
Fall and fumble
Get lost and go blind

Come dance with clouds
See further yet
There's no limit, no end
Don't forget
We'll be around
Our spirits free

Completely close, forever
You and me

West of Sky
East of stars
A sacred place lies
The here and now
When we breathe together
The sea opens up
Whirlwind water fire
There is no beginning, no stop

Come dance with clouds
See further yet
There's no limit, no end
Don't forget
We'll be around
Our spirits free
Completely close, forever
You and me

"The Never-Ending Hunger" by Laura Hemenway

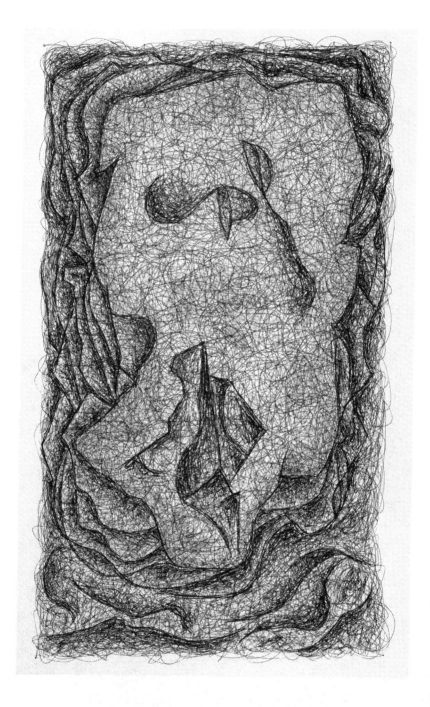

"Untitled April 27, 2016" by Stephen T. Vessels

DOWN THE RABBIT HOLE

WITH

STEPHEN T. VESSELS

SCOTCH AND THE QUEEN OF CUPS: CARTOMANCY WITH STEPHEN T. VESSELS

by Silver Webb

They say you can tell a lot about a person by their choice of cocktail, and Stephen is very definite on this topic.

"I only drink scotch."

He also wears a fedora, smokes American Spirits, and sports a rakish goatee. I imagine he is actually Ernest Hemingway, somehow spit forward in the time stream and now driven to write lyric, dark stories that are "a mashup of science-fiction, fantasy, and horror."

Sitting down to a pub list of 30+ kinds of scotch, I test the beverage prospects.

"So, will there be mitigating factors?" I ask.

"Such as?" he inquires.

"Water? Bubbles?" *Don't people order scotch and tonic?*

"One does not put impurities in the water of life," he says with the calm of an emperor about to give a thumbs-down in the Colosseum.

I'm pretty sure that means even ice cubes aren't a thing for a scotch connoisseur. We settle on a Balvenie that is twenty-one years old. Old enough to know what it's doing, I suppose, old enough to be legal in a bar. It's a delight to drink something so smooth and deadly; a good combination to start an interview. To counter, or perhaps augment, the beverage, I pull out my tarot deck. To his credit, Stephen's eyes only bulge a little as I ask him to pick a card.

I suppose by now he must realize I don't believe in boring interviews. But I do have a reason for the tarot. Stephen's novel, *Door of Tireless Pursuit*, is based on a tarot game called *Dungeon Solitaire: Labyrinth of Souls*, designed by Matthew Lowes. A group of writers that Stephen met in Eugene, Oregon, have banded together, each taking a turn writing a novel based on this tarot, novels like *Littlest Death*, *The End of All Things*, and *Benediction Denied*. Stephen's first contribution to this series came out in October 2017.

But as Stephen flips a card now, it seems this conversation will be led by the Queen of cups. A regal figure gazing thoughtfully into the waters of the psyche, expressing herself clearly and deeply. The first portent of the evening. The second involves a python, but more on that later.

I actually saw Stephen speaking, not too long ago, at the Santa Barbara Writer's Conference, where he acts as a mentor and manuscript consultant to attendees. It's his manner to encourage other writers as much as possible, and he told the audience, when asked about the value of conferences, "They have been critical for me. I recommend them strongly. They can be terribly expensive, so you have to moderate how much of that you do. I don't go looking for the big break, the connection I'm going to make that will solve all my problems. I go as a perpetual student. And all the people there (ThrillerFest or Worldcon) who have succeeded don't have to tell people why they're there. By and large, writers who write about horrible things are very decent, kind-hearted, generous, open people. I have found that to be almost universally the case. Everything that has happened to me has happened because of the friendships I've made in the writing community. So I encourage you to go out and make those friendships as broadly as you can. You'll want to get published so that everyone else will feel like they can go out and get published."

Personally, I find the feedback, if not the encouragement and company of other writers to be crucial to writing. And Stephen agrees, "The breaks for me, as I see them, have been the people I've connected with. Squirreling myself away with my work for a long time was the biggest mistake I've ever made. Being out in a community of writers, the writers in my life, those were my big breaks. Without that, this book [*The Door of Tireless Pursuit*] wouldn't exist. The first big break I got was getting work published in the *Ellery Queen Mystery Magazine.* Having something like that happen doesn't mean you're jumping into wild success immediately. But it's very important for writers to get published. Not necessarily a Big 5 publisher, but just having a hard copy you can hold onto is the finalization of a very hard, long process."

The short story he published in *Ellery Queen* was one of twelve he wrote that were eventually gathered and published in the 2016 anthology *The Mountain and the*

Vortex. He published two books in two years, in fact. My take on the appeal of his prose is that he is playing with symbols and meanings based in myth and the subconscious, but he doesn't hit you over the head with it. You are somehow left with the subtle feeling that the author designed each story with the intention of guiding you toward a realization or at least leaving you with a meaningful question. I ask him if this is intentional construction or something that flows out without consideration.

"It's a little hard to talk about this because it's amorphous for me. I have done a fair amount of reading of Jung, Campbell, the usual suspects. If I'm applying a symbol, rather than trying to call up a specific reference for a reader, it's more like I'm diving down into the mulch of symbology and semiotics and following my intuition and my ear. Because I'm not allied with a specific delineation of forces and forms. So I'm sort of getting them to dance with each other."

But I'm not quite certain I believe him, so I go in for a second pass, "In your short stories, a common theme is that a character goes on a physical journey, either down into a subterranean space, or into the woods. These are classic mythological tropes for entering the subconscious. Was that intentional?"

He only cracks half way. "Yeah, I would say yes. Although again, I'm not a respecter of categories or delineations. I do have a sense that we're connected in ways that we don't recognize, whether it's electrically or etherical or due to how our cultures have evolved out of organic and pre-organic circumstances. I ferret around inside myself and I see something like what I want and then I keep looking at it differently until it becomes something unique in a specific way that gets me in my gut."

Stephen's gut is not leading him astray. But American Spirits may well be. He steps out for a smoke, and I look at my notes, wondering how to better lure out the raconteur. I ponder that he is a Wood Goat in the Chinese zodiac and a Cancer in the European. These two things together might suggest that he is intensely loyal and likable, with deep emotions. I pick my own tarot card and up pops Virtue. Virtue, indeed. This means, definitively, it is time for another round of scotch. This time a thirteen-year-old Craigellachie. I do wonder where Stephen has gotten to. It seems he might be smoking three or four cigarettes for the time he's been gone...perhaps an entire cigar. Just as the scotch arrives in a pretty tulip glass, I look up and see Stephen waving from the door of the patio with what looks like an anaconda over his shoulders. I do my level best not to shriek. There is definitely something hissy and deadly wrapped around his neck. Its little black tongue is flicking at me. Apparently "cigarette break" is a euphemism for cavorting with snakes. I slither into the shadows of the booth and get a head start on the second round.

"A very friendly snake," he says on his return, smiling like he's met Arthur Miller. I resist the urge to spritz him with antibacterial spray. Possibly the fumes from the scotch will have the same effect anyway.

As portents go, snakes range from terror to temptation, and occassionally divination...think of a priestess holding snakes above her in a temple. Snakes are also escape artists and known to slip the skin. To wit, if you learn anything from this interview about Stephen, let it be that he should not be left alone too long, lest he run off to join the circus.

The Craigellachie is a pleasant little ball of flame in my throat, and I skip straight past all of the interview questions that look rather mundane now. Here's a good one: "Hungry, wandering ghosts show up in at least two of your stories. Why is that?"

He ponders his glass. "I hadn't intended to drift off into cosmology, but I do have a sense that there is a non-corporeal aspect to being that extends beyond physical death. That has been supported for me by experiences I've had. That doesn't mean that I have any idea what that reality is like. I have the same reaction to a uniformly blissful or transportive notion of an afterlife as I do to notions that reality isn't that simple. I like to play with the supernatural. I've never been happy or satisfied with depictions of the afterlife that have been given to me by science or religion. I notice holes in reasoning sometimes, and I figure since none of the existing answers seem to gel for me, I may as well make them up myself. I like dealing with the unknown and running smack up against it, because it has this sense of expanding the scope of experience."

So when I ask him who his literary influences are, I'm expecting an arcane list of philosophy books. I'm betting on the Esperanto Bible, *Sergei Bulgakov's Sorrows*, and *The Lost Codex of St. Angus*. Instead, I hear "*Little Women, Nancy Drew, Middlemarch,* and *Treasure Island.*" He amends quickly with a more adult list: Isaac Asimov, Philip K. Dick, and Ursula K. Le Guin, among others. But he circles around with "I think it's significant to me that I still remember *Little Women*. Why? I guess the passion. Jo and the professor. And her sister dying, which still gets me. Who gets to say these things aren't real?

They're real to me."

I understand this well. The characters I write are very real to me. They keep me company. Sometimes they are better company than the nonfictional people in my life. I mention this to Stephen, and he replies, "Jun'ichirō Tanazaki said that his characters came to life and he had to write their stories so they would leave him the hell alone. And it does feel like that sometimes. I don't feel like I'm writing about hypothetical characters, and there comes a point where what I think should happen becomes less important to me than what's true for them."

You might think from hearing him speak that Stephen has been writing continuously his whole life. But in fact, although he first wanted to write when he was a young boy, it was not until his mid-fifties that he started to have publication success, and he admits, "I fell fallow for periods. I had some misconceptions. Probably the biggest one was that I had to pass through some kind of membrane of learning and experience in order to write, which is utter nonsense. I was waiting for the planets to align. It took me a long time to disabuse myself of the notion that inspiration had some special moment where the words would come to me. If there's a break in your writing where you lose your facility, it takes a few weeks to get it back. That should be said to every writer: It takes about two weeks to get back in the groove and thirty days to form a habit. Now it's true for me that I need to be creating something every day."

That daily work ethic is coming to fruition. He is writing two novels that will be published in the coming year, one of which will be a second installment in the *Labyrinth of*

Souls.

The interview seems to be winding down. While there's time, shall I tell you all his secrets? Very well. Stephen is passionate about classical music (see Arsentiy Kharitonov's site masterpiecefinder.com, to which Stephen contributes) and a talented artist (this volume is generously peppered with his drawings). He also writes his manuscripts by hand and texts by slowly booping at the screen with one finger. A Luddite, he says. Stephen may be gregarouis with a booming voice that fills the room, but so too is he ruminative, introspective. I suspect the man at home writing is very different than the man holding court in the pub. But most good writers are this way. To slip the veil, journey to the feral, broken places of the psyche, and bring back stories to the page is not always the task of the happy. Although, if you are a happy and prolific writer, brava to you. Perhaps you'll come buy us a scotch? There's a really nice snake here, I'm told.

"Rougette and Stephen, Lest You Doubt"

FROM DUST RETURNED

by Stephen T. Vessels

The following is the opening chapter from a novel-in-progress.

Wretched and defiant, Miriam climbed the hill.

Wind whipped at her funeral gown and splayed the deep grass in sheets. At the top stood sanctuary, incomprehensible in its abrupt presence, the house her father had built, with its steep, gable roof, broad porch, large windows upstairs and down, and an oculus centering the attic. Somehow, she had made her way home.

She wondered if her father's ship had arrived. Visions of catastrophe circled its absence; it was days late reaching the port. He would want to know what had happened to her, and she feared to tell him. He would seek revenge, and he was too old to battle a bully. She only wanted his kind, welcoming smile, his sheltering embrace, his quiet voice reassuring her that she was safe and all would be well. He would help her to her room and they would pray together, and he would stroke her hair and sing to her softly until she fell asleep. The loss of her mother never left his eyes. She loved him for continuing to grieve.

Miriam did not know how she had come here. The last thing she remembered was the faceless brute thrusting her to the cobbles and bearing down through a miasma of whiskey and sweat. She stopped and looked back across the water, met a startling expanse of lights that could not be Boston dimming the stars in the sky. The inlet was too narrow. White, behemoth conveyances of some kind, with what looked like mammoth wings sticking out of them, stood on a broad, paved spur of land on the other side, some moving about with a purpose Miriam did not comprehend.

Something about the house was strange, too—many things, the more she looked. She couldn't be sure of colors in darkness, but the house had never been green. The sash windows, fitted with large panes of plate glass, should have been mullioned. The old elm whose shade she cherished for reading was gone. Other trees, equally venerable but wrong in their placement and too many in number, confused the lay of the grounds. The carriage house was fitted out like a small cottage. A flat-roofed, wall-less shed stood where the paddocks should have been, a curious motor car sheltering beneath it.

Shrieking thunder tore the air. In contradiction of all that was natural, one of the winged behemoths descended from the sky. She tried to scream but had no voice; stared in terrified wonder as the impossible thing came to ground across the water.

She ran to the house, tried to open the front door but couldn't grasp the knob. She beat with both hands but her blows made no sound. She stepped back, gaping. The etched glass oval in the door she knew, but the vision through it afforded bewildering vacancies. The standing clock was there, but the coat rack was missing, as was the sideboard where she kept her mother's tea set displayed on a lace table runner. Where the floral throw rug, imported at great expense from Italy, should have been, polished floorboards lay exposed.

She tried again to open the door. Not only could she not grip the knob, she could not feel it in her hand. She ran her thumb across her fingertips. She could not feel anything.

She closed her eyes and stood still, mastering her panic. She needed to get inside the house. She needed her father. She needed him to explain what was happening. She opened her eyes, striving to remain calm.

The door knocker, too, was missing. The more she looked anywhere the more disoriented she became.

There was a white button to the right of the door frame. Miriam squinted at it, unsure of its purpose.

Detective Cyril Palmer poured bourbon into a coffee mug and sat back down at the dining room table to continue reviewing the file. The wind howling around the house did not distract him, though he was pricked with homesickness. Denver would be white with winter, but here in Boston the first snows had yet to fall. He read through witness statements, pinching the flesh under his lips between forefinger and thumb. Photos of the victim poked up from the back of the file—the bloody scalp and bruised forehead. Claudia Hiller had been beaten so badly she might never wake up. Not by the college boy the rest of the unit liked for it. Owen Rainer was too soft, too naive. There'd been no hidden smile in his eyes, only misery. They were looking for someone who made brutality a vocation.

Cyril's gut certainty would not eliminate Rainer as a suspect. The circumstantial evidence against him was damning. He knew the victim; he'd attended classes with her, argued with her, and been seen near where she was found. It fell to Cyril to find a fly in another ointment. Instinct told him that this was not an isolated act but the work of someone smart and practiced who enjoyed frustrating the police as much as he did hurting women.

The doorbell rang. Cyril couldn't imagine who would come at this hour. He took his service pistol from its holster on the table, stuck it in the back of his slacks, and went to the foyer. He saw no one through the glass oval.

A transient scent of dank earth grazed his nostrils as he opened the door.

"Hello?"

Wind tossed the branches of the maple, pine, and mimosa trees around the house, and the laurel bushes flanking the porch. Across the inlet, the lights of Boston beckoned like a knobbly carpet of jewels. Cyril pulled out his gun and made a circuit of the house and grounds. The only car under the carport was his aging Toyota; the long driveway was empty. He checked the guest house. The door was locked, the windows securely shut. Maybe he'd imagined the bell. His auditory hallucinations were usually vocal, but sometimes he heard other things.

He went back inside, sat a moment at the dining table, listening. He grimaced and returned to his notes. He pulled the photos out of the file and spread them on the table. A plane passed overhead with a muted roar and a wailing moan rose behind him. Cyril snatched the gun from the table and spun around. He caught a fleeting impression of a human figure, like a dispersing coalescence of mist. The moan faded in a cresting wave and there was no one there.

He searched the house, checked the doors, stopped at the foot of the stairs in the entry hall. Right then and there he decided to schedule an appointment with a neurologist.

He grabbed the bourbon from the kitchen on his way back to the dining table, drained what was in the mug, and poured himself more. He stared sightlessly at his notes. His uncle had had a brain tumor, and Cyril's genetic history placed him at risk for the same. He'd heard things when he was young. Since he'd come out of his coma it had started again.

Pressure grew in Cyril's ears, as if he rose sharply in altitude. He frowned and rubbed them. The standing clock in the entry chimed midnight. The pressure released.

"What happened here?" a voice asked.

Goosebumps scaled Cyril's flesh and his pulse quickened. A woman in a white dress with a lacy bodice sat across from him, her hair done up on top of her head in a fat Victorian bun. The impression of supernatural phenomenon warred with fears for his mind. "You're not real."

The woman raised her chin and her expression stiffened. She had narrow features and sterling eyes. Something about her was familiar.

"Well, I see you and you seem to see me," she replied.

The standing clock, with rapid rattles and clicks, made a noisy shift in its cycle. Cyril looked at it.

"That is my father's clock," the woman said. "It is the only thing in this house familiar to me, though I know that I lived here. I use the preterite because I'm having the impression that I'm dead."

The urge to flee yielded to the inner poise Cyril asserted in moments of danger. He experimented with voicing his foremost thought: "You're a ghost?"

She turned her head toward the window at the far end of the living room and gazed into the windblown night. "Either that or I'm having an especially vivid dream, which somehow I doubt."

"Or I have a brain tumor."

Her attention came back to Cyril. "That might explain our circumstances if yours were the only perspective at issue." She folded her hands on the table. "I lived in this house in 1907. This does not feel like 1907."

"It's . . . 2017."

A tear leaked from the woman's eye. She wiped it away with a trembling hand. "That is horrifying." Another airliner passed overhead; she looked up fearfully.

By reflex part male and part defensive, Cyril sought to reassure her. "It's just a plane landing. We're near the airport."

Her expression exhibited incomprehension.

"You're safe."

The woman scowled. "How can you possibly know that?"

Cyril drew back, scalded. "What do you want? Why are you here?" If he indulged her, maybe the part of his mind that produced her would unclench and release him to sanity.

The woman frowned, scanning the table. "Why are you looking at those hideous pictures?"

Cyril had learned to ignore the ugliness of such images. Maybe long-suppressed loathing had surfaced as an apparition. He did not want to converse with a figment of his mind. Every word he uttered felt like a step down the rabbit hole of madness.

The awkwardness of withholding response was more daunting. He cleared his throat. "I'm a police officer. They relate to a case I'm investigating."

The woman continued to stare. "The girl was murdered?"

Cyril remembered his mother showing him old pictures in an album. An idea who the woman might be came to him, and he wondered, against all reason, if she could be real. "She's hanging by a thread."

"Was she . . . interfered with?"

Cyril remembered a particular picture, an oval portrait, old and faded, in a worn and creased card-stock frame. A name came to him. "She was raped, yes."

The woman inhaled sharply. "I am understanding my memories better. I believe that I was . . . raped . . . and killed."

The air in the room thickened. The woman's dress and manner were antiquated. The more Cyril studied her, the more she agreed with the likeness in his memory. He downed more bourbon. Whether addressed to himself or a bonafide spook, the question wanted answering. "If it's all right, may I ask who you are?"

The woman blinked. "Of course it's all right. My name is Miriam Summerspoon."

Cyril swallowed. Either he'd gone mad or the world had. "My mother had a photo of you. When you were . . . younger, I think. You're my great . . . great—" he didn't know how many 'greats' were involved—"aunt." He finished the whiskey in the mug.

"And you are?"

"Your . . . nephew. I guess. Cyril Palmer." He wished he hadn't identified himself.

A gust of wind rattled the windows. Cyril had a sudden taste of salt in his mouth.

The woman appraised him differently. "Do I frighten you?"

Cyril had faced a gun several times, and been shot twice. He didn't know what was aiming at him, now. He knew only one way to meet fear. If a black dog chased you, you didn't wait for it to catch up to turn around. He made himself relax, regarding what his senses told him was the living ghost of his great aunt. "No," he said finally. It surprised him, how true it felt. On the other hand, if she were real . . . "I want to know what's going on."

The wind thrashed the laurels beneath the window at his back. Cyril felt the emptiness of the house, the distance from people he had chosen.

"Yes," Miriam said. "Something brought me here."

"Maybe we should . . ." He didn't know how to finish the thought. She looked entirely physical. Not transparent, like in movies.

"Try to understand?" she finished for him. She looked again at the photographs, reached for one. "May I?"

Mystery acquired new layers. He gestured permission.

She picked up a picture of the strangulation bruises on the rape victim's throat. Physical, then, Cyril thought, watching her hold the photo and scrutinize it. She picked up another, of the gash in the victim's scalp.

"Who is she?"

"I can't discuss the details of an ongoing—" Cyril stopped. There were no provisions governing conversations with imaginary persons. He took a long breath. "A college student."

"Poor girl." Miriam frowned at the photos. "Which came first, do you think, the blow or the choking?"

Cyril's brow rose. "That's a good question."

"Is it?" Miriam was surprised.

He took another steadying breath and gestured at the photo she held. His hand shook. "The blow probably knocked her out." He was conversing with an hallucination like a colleague. He steadied himself with the investigative attitude to which he was habituated. "He hit her with something hard and narrow, like a pipe or a baton. Assuming he strangled her while he raped her, if she was unconscious it suggests a fixation with the act."

"You mean that it was personal."

The rabbit hole was behind him. He'd arrived at the Mad Hatter's for tea. "Not necessarily."

She watched him, waiting for him to go on.

He cleared his throat again. "She could represent someone else to him, or an idea he has about women. Either way, if she was unconscious, it takes the act beyond rape. Most rapists want their victims to know what's happening to them."

"They want to see them suffer."

"They want to exert control over them."

Miriam studied the photographs. "And do you know which came first?"

"The examining physician thinks the blow. There's no indication Claudia struggled."

"Perhaps she was too frightened to fight back."

"With rape that's possible. Strangulation, everyone fights."

Miriam picked up another photo. "Do you know how I died, Cyril?"

Of all the questions he had ever been asked . . . "My mother said you were murdered."

She held his gaze, nodded, looked inward. "That explains it."

"What?"

She glanced around the house. "Did you inherit it?"

"It came on the market. I just moved in." With debt for the rest of his life.

"You have no pictures on the walls."

The emptiness of the place registered in a way it hadn't before. He didn't even have a sofa or an armchair. His failure with Stephanie had left him little interest in creature comforts.

"I sense you live alone," Miriam said. "Forgive me, you seem old not to be married."

"My fiancé changed her mind."

Miriam cocked her head in query.

"I was shot. She couldn't handle it." The old shame that told him he deserved to be lonely took a swipe at him. He was made for the company of ghosts.

Miriam studied a full body shot of the victim. "Do you think I'm here because of this?"

"The thought's crossing my mind," he murmured.

"That maybe . . . I'm supposed to help you."

"I don't know."

"Could there be a connection? Between what happened to me and this child?"

"You died a hundred years ago."

Miriam's focus turned inward again. "All I remember is being attacked." She shook her head. "Then nothing."

The detective in Cyril made an inchoate link between memory and estrangement. "You mean, maybe the same thing happened to you. Maybe you were knocked unconscious, raped, and left for dead."

"I'd like to know," she said softly. Her voice had a soothing quality, like purling water.

Cyril scanned the photos of Claudia Hiller's humiliation. He couldn't see a connection but sensed there was one. It was strong, like another presence in the room. Miriam seemed entirely physical and alive. Nothing about her gave any indication of someone insubstantial or ethereal. "You don't look like a ghost."

"I . . . don't feel like one, I think. Not that I know what a ghost should feel like."

Beneath fear of madness, beneath dread of dying,

beneath judgement and the horror of the unknown, lay another sense, an aspiration, a hope, hidden, suppressed, dormant, somehow, long dormant—protected, maybe, in secret even from himself, for releasing it to the full flush of awareness would render him vulnerable. Cyril swallowed. It would not be suppressed: awe, child wonder, the indefensible certainty that life was more than it seemed rose in him like a spring breaking the surface. His whole body vibrated with it, the possibility that she could be real; that he, tiny he, wretched he, could be in the presence of something beyond what was known and measurable and assumed, something that defied explanation, that broke the walls of defeat and disillusionment and crushed cynicism.

"Can I—may I touch you?"

Miriam's eyebrows rose. Cyril put forth his hand and she stared at it. Hesitantly, she placed her fingers on his palm.

Cyril felt more than her touch. A force swept through him, banishing doubt. He saw Miriam's eyes widen as she caught her breath. She felt it too.

The words that came out of him had no thought behind them. They were propelled by a rush of emotion. "You are welcome here, Miriam Summerspoon. This is your home."

Miriam gripped Cyril's hand and wept. "Oh, nephew. My dear nephew."

THE DOOR OF TIRELESS PURSUIT: A REVIEW

by Chris Wozney

When C. S. Lewis wrote an introduction for his allegorical fantasy, *The Pilgrim's Regress*, he defined eight distinct elements of Romanticism; Vessels' debut novel contains all eight, and even a ninth that Lewis, rather characteristically, left out. *The Door of Tireless Pursuit* is a tale of dangerous adventure in remote places (definition 1); it is peopled by strange beings wielding marvelous powers who hold to codes of honor (definitions 2 and 3); some events are macabre (definition 4); there is serious exploration of the limits of egoism and subjectivism (definition 5); the antagonist's revolt against the existing order qualifies for definition 6; the sensibility to nature, while not as rhyming as Wordsworth's, answers for definition 7; and oh, most certainly, Stephen Vessels conveys the romanticism of intense longing, of "Sweet Desire." This he does inimically, better perhaps, than Lewis himself. The title and the section headings are all indicative of this: Part One is "The School of a Thousand Dreams," Part Two "The Lair of Rapturous Delights," Part Three "The Desert of Languorous Torments." Ninthly, there is an actual romance between the two main characters, something Lewis usually eschewed in his own fictional writings. (The only marriage I can recall is the one between Aravis and Cor at the end of *The Horse and His Boy*, and that one only took place so they could fight and make up more conveniently. An instructive example, but hardly a romantic one.) It is this ninth order of romance that catapults the protagonist into his strange adventure.

Alexander "Sandy" Creaze has an ordinary life, and a good one by ordinary standards: work, friendships, a home in L.A., hobbies. A chance meeting with a beautiful woman named Lark and a step into the unknown changes his life forever. In a single evening he learns that there are doorways in time and space that one can pass through if one is quick enough, that some who are quick gather for camaraderie and the occasional brawl in a bar beneath New York City, and that fear can cost you more than your anger can redeem.

When the smoke and dust clear, Lark is missing and Sandy finds himself back in his own place and time. He sets out, determined to discover if what he experienced was actual or a delusion. The counsel of an old friend and some basic detective work convince Sandy that weird can indeed be real.

Precipitous violence and threats have the opposite effect on Sandy than was intended: instead of scaring him off, they make him more resolved than ever to figure out what the hell is going on, and why a singular woman is at the heart of all the conflict.

Choice by choice, by steps, leaps, and sometimes by falls, Sandy penetrates a strange, vast labyrinth of marvels and terrors, encounters dragons, monarchs, monsters, trackless deserts, and true allies, and is tested beyond the boundaries of his endurance.

Eventually, understanding Lark's own quest becomes as important to Sandy as finding her again; because while love can show you in an instant who you want to be with, only understanding shows you how to be with them.

There is an ineffable quality to Vessels' storytelling that is reminiscent of George MacDonald's best work: *The Princess and Curdie, Lilith*, and *Phantastes*. Vessels is adept at the transition from ordinary life to the extraordinary, which is the heartstone of fantasy. This novel has horrific elements, but these are balanced out by moments of humor, instances of kindness, and lightning-bright epiphanies. It can certainly be enjoyed as an escapist adventure, but it can also savored as a well-crafted, complex example of a hero's journey that is all the more compelling for him seeming to be, at first, so unlike a hero. And I appreciate that other characters also have complexity and depth, not only the protagonist. Several who are little more than cameo appearances are nonetheless uniquely memorable. There is the one entity who is... profoundly disturbing, in an intriguing, I'd-like-to-encounter-you-again-but-only-vicariously kind of way. And according to the author, some of these characters will reappear in his next *Labyrinth of Souls* novel, due out in 2019.

In terms of wordcraft, Vessels is a genius, no getting around that. His writing reminds me of Lord Dunsany,

Roger Zelazny, and Harlan Ellison, yet at the same time is completely original. Phrases of foreshadowing are so subtly delivered that you have to look back with hindsight to spot some of them. There are passages that render me awestruck by how absolutely right he gets a voice, a feeling, a moment, an exchange of dialogue. No one writes this well from mere imagination; you have to have lived some of it, and you have to have a genuine appreciation for, love for, the diversity of creatures in this world and all its alternatives.

As for the remarkable cover, the image is "Inner Desert," one of twelve new Major Arcana designed by Matthew Lowes and illustrated by Joseph Vandel for *The Labyrinth of Souls*, a card game that is part D&D, part solitaire, played with a 90-card expansion of the tarot deck. *The Door of Tireless Pursuit* is the fifth stand-alone publication based on Lowes' game. Each writer selects a card and composes a story inspired by that picture. More than one participating author has based their story on an actual game played with the deck, or a tarot spread done with the cards. Vessels' story includes a number of tarot cards personified as characters, or as aspects of characters in times of crisis. It is exhilarating to spot these manifestations, all the more so as they tend to have a seismic effect on the unfolding plot.

Author, editor, and publisher Christina Lay has this to say of the project: "*The Labyrinth of Souls*…is a mythic underworld, existing at a crossroads of people and cultures, between time and space, between the physical world and the deepest reaches of the psyche. It is a dark mirror held up to human experience, in which you may find your dreams…or your doom." Six novels thusfar exist in the series: *Benediction*

Denied by Elizabeth Engstrom, *Symphony of Ruin* by Christina Lay, *The End of All Things* by Matthew Lowes, *Littlest Death* by Eric M. Witchey (recipient of the Independent Publishers Silver Medal Award for Fantasy), and *The Snake's Song* by Mary E. Lowd. The project is ongoing, with *Mountain of Ashes* by John R. Reed forthcoming.

My compliments to Shadow Spinners Press, for the books themselves are small masterpieces of workmanship. The pages have the density of high rag content, the line spacing is very kind to the eyes. They are the sort of books that hands are happy to hold, reluctant to relinquish. Especially when they are as intensely readable as *The Door of Tireless Pursuit*.

Expanded from a review published in The Nameless Zine, *June 2018.*

THE MOUNTAIN & THE VORTEX AND OTHER TALES: A REVIEW

by Chris Wozney

These stories, in the horror and speculative fiction genres, are narrated with a restraint that lets horror bloom in the mind of the reader only as a result of the reader's own comprehension, and astonishment dawning like sunrise over the ocean. More than one of these stories was like seeing a green flash of the most startling imagination. The illustrations, by Vessels himself, Steven C. Gilberts, Alan M. Clark, Cheryl Owen-Wilson, and Jean Giraud Moebius, are phenomenal; the hardback edition contains additional artwork by Clark.

Each story stands alone, and yet there are themes, images, even single words that make bridges spun of diamonds and darkness that connect one story to another, and yet another. Their progressive coherence makes *The Mountain and the Vortex* a sort of modern-day *Tales of the Thousand Nights* and *One Night*. The beginning is grim; the author is looking into the heart of the worst of human possibilities, just as *The Arabian Nights* begins with the worst sort of abuse of power. Vessels, like Scheherazade, gradually introduces elements of courage in the midst of despair, hope, humor, and love. In some instances, this only makes the horror more appalling; another quality shared by both collections. At the conclusion of *The Arabian Nights*, the Sultan has been transformed, some might say redeemed, by the stories Scheherazade has told him. After reading the stories Vessels has presented, I felt harrowed, but hallowed as well, and I had a great deal more sympathy for that Sultan, because for the first time I felt that he and I had something in common; we had both been schooled.

If you wish to discover these for yourself entirely on your own terms, you may prefer to skip the brief descriptions that follow. If you like previews, read on! I will not, however, tease out the marvelous threads that tie one tale to another; it would be mean-spirited to rob you of your epiphanies.

"No Night, No Need of Candle" is purest horror, a Dante-esque post-apocalyptic landscape of souls who have abandoned all hope and are abandoned to their terrible fate. (C. S. Lewis would have loved this one!)

"The Butcher of Gad Street" has an unlikely hero who, to rescue his daughter, must defeat demons who have been systematically enthralling humans and tainting supernatural energies.

"Lighter than Air" is a true märchen, in which dreary, deadly ordinariness is transformed into something wonderful, only here the magic is an act of spirit. Lester Gill is dying, and he's morbidly obese; then he decides to ... let go.

"Bulbous Things" is military SF/horror of the first water. As a team of scientists and their single military guardian explore a planet with a singular life form, the question is, which life form is studying which, and how? Fair warning: after reading this one, there may be times when you see the world through the narrator's eyes and persona; if you are not okay with sharing your brain space with a quasi-psychotic muscle-neck, you may want to be careful with this one. Active duty and prior service readers will feel right at home.

"The Burning Professor" is a fantasy parable that burns through so much crap it might as well be written in letters of white fire on black fire. It may seem like a feminist story, but it is a story for everyone old enough to have regrets, or wise enough to know they will someday, regardless of present age. Women enjoy and benefit from countless tales with male protagonists; surely men can do as much with a lady protagonist.

"Doloroso" is a modern western of the drug-smuggling border, absolutely realistic, if you allow for a ghostly visitation.

"Dining Strange" is a splendid mix of Poe-ish revenge and science fiction realpolitik, as a galactic ambassador brings hard justice to a planetary government and its allies who have played favorites at his expense.

"Verge Land" is pure mischief: take a horror trope so familiar it is a cliché, then go all weird with it. The way the horizons blur and merge into a Mobius strip reminds me of Robert Louis Stevenson's fantasy tale of a princess on a shore.

"The Alchemist's Eyeglasses" is more of a romantic romp, but the bubbling questions and issues of integrity, courage, and living blindly or with foreknowledge are real posers. An argumentative group of friends could have fun with this one for hours.

"Significance" is a darker sort of mischief; Loki in destructive mode. Certainly a warning, possibly a predictive, it is a reminder that nobody causes disaster like smart, fearful people with hubris and military-grade technology.

"The Fourth Seven" is classic horror, Stephen King horror, where banal, human evil and supernatural evil conspire, and human decency has only a small chance to salvage anything from the cesspit.

The titular novella that closes out the book is a philosophical fantasy that reminded me of an obscure classic by George MacDonald called "The Golden Key." Since I verified the author had never even heard of that story, let alone read it, I conclude that archetypal forces are at work. MacDonald's story was for children; apparently, archetypal forces deem humanity mature enough for an adult version. "The Mountain and the Vortex" is one of those cinematic stories that you see unfolding in your mind's eye, as if some amazing director had just planted his rear in your hippocampus and taken over the direction of your waking dreams, with the aid of some naturally occurring psychotropics.

Each story, no matter how fantastic, is grounded in the truth of "this is how nature is, this is how people are." Some fantastic representations of philosophical ideas may be so accurate that a reader encounters them with a shock of recognition: "I know this! I felt this, but I didn't have the words for what it was I was feeling!" Or the ideas may be familiar—Zelazy and Lackey have used similar representations in some of their tales—expressed in a new form. Either way, every single story in this volume is an adventure. Another plus: the puns are subtle and clever enough that readers who hate puns can loftily ignore them, while connoisseurs can score points for detecting them.

To sum up this book, let me say that never in my life have I encountered such depth and poignancy of imagination. Vessels seems to have distilled the essence of Harlan Ellison, Lovecraft, Zelazny, other influences I cannot identify, and certainly something of himself, to produce a brandy the gods would savour. These are the stories I have been looking for all my adult life.

First published in The Nameless Zine, *May 2016*

Contributors

CONTRIBUTORS

Cathryn Beeks

Cathryn is a singer/songwriter and show host for Listen Local where she shares the stories, music, and art of local movers and shakers in San Diego. You can visit her at www. cathrynbeeks.com.

Donna Lynn Caskey

Donna Lynn is an innovative clawhammer "Banjo Gal," as she is known, and so much more. A strong songwriter, her work simultaneously acknowledges life's difficulties and offers a genuine message of hope. Her sound retains a timeless quality that hearkens back to traditional old-time mountain music and bluegrass while artfully exploring contemporary subject matter as demonstrated on her two albums, *Nameless Heart* and *The Love Still Shows*. Audiences appreciate Donna Lynn's heartfelt, playful, and engaging stage presence and the opportunity to sing along during performances. For more information, please go to www.donnalynncaskey.com.

Lisa Cheby

Lisa's poems, articles, and reviews have appeared in various journals including *The Rumpus, Entropy, Knowledge Quest, The Citron Review, Tidal Basin Review, A cappella Zoo,* and *TAB: Journal of Poetry and Poetics,* which nominated her poem for a 2015 Pushcart Prize. Lisa's poems are also found in the anthologies *Drawn to Marvel, The Burden of Light,* and *Coiled Serpent.* Her chapbook, *Love Lessons from Buffy the Vampire Slayer* (Dancing Girl Press) was featured in The Wardrobe's Best Dressed Series. Lisa holds an MFA from Antioch University and an MLIS from SJSU. lisacheby.wordpress.com

Ted Chiles

Ted came to creative writing after moving to California in 2003. With a Ph.D. in Economics, he taught economics at the undergraduate and graduate levels. In 2013, he completed an MFA in fiction from Spalding University. Chiles' fiction has been published in print and online and consists of short stories and flash fiction. His style varies from realism to magical realism to speculative fiction. He also has published creative nonfiction, adapted a novella for the stage, and written two ten-minute plays, one of which was produced in Santa Barbara. Originally from the Rust Belt, Chiles lives in Santa Barbara with a writer and two cats.

Nina Clements

Nina earned an MFA in creative writing from Sarah Lawrence College and is the author of the chapbook *Set the Table,* from Finishing Line Press. She currently lives in Ventura, California, and works as a librarian.

Chella Courington

Chella is a writer and teacher. With a Ph.D. in American and British Literature and an MFA in Poetry, she is the author of five poetry and four flash fiction chapbooks. Her poetry and flash fiction appear in numerous anthologies and journals, including *The Los Angeles Review*, *Spillway*, *SmokeLong Quarterly*, and *The Collagist*. Originally from the Appalachian South, Courington lives in California with another writer and two cats. For more information, visit chellacourington.net.

Cyrus Cromwell

Cyrus has a deep and abiding love for the way fantasy fiction delivers both author and reader to the depths of their imagination. The forthcoming *Born of Fire* is his debut novel in the genre and the first in the *Shadow Dragons Trilogy*. You can visit him at www.cyruscromwell.com.

Gwen Dandridge

Gwen Dandridge is a writer of young adult and middle-grade novels. She is also a lover of golden retrievers, maker of excellent pastries, breads, and funky art. You can visit her website at www.gwendandridge.com.

Nicholas Deitch

Nick is a writer, teacher, architect, and activist. Originally from Los Angeles, California, he now lives in Ventura, with his wife, Diana. He is an annual participant at the Santa Barbara Writer's Conference. He has been published in the London literary journal, *Litro*, and is currently writing his first novel, *Death and Life in the City of Dreams*, a story about a dying city and those who struggle to save it.

Kim Dower

Kim, originally from New York City, is the author of three collections of poetry, all from Red Hen Press, with a forthcoming collection, *Sunbathing on Tyrone Power's Grave*, due out on April 1, 2019. Kim was the City Poet Laureate of West Hollywood from October, 2016–October, 2018. Kim's work has been nominated for two Pushcarts and has been featured in the Academy of American Poets, Poem-A-Day, "The Writer's Almanac," and "American Life in Poetry," as well as in *Ploughshares, Barrow Street, Rattle,* and *Eclipse.* Her poems are included in several anthologies. She teaches poetry workshops in the B.A. Program of Antioch University.

Yvonne M. Estrada

Yvonne is a poet and photographer. Her chapbook, *My Name on Top of Yours*, is a crown of sonnets that explores graffiti and includes original photographs. Her poems have recently appeared in *Talking Writing* and *Fourth and Main* and are anthologized in *Wide Awake: Poets of Los Angeles and Beyond* and *Coiled Serpent: Poets Arising from the Cultural Quakes and Shifts of Los Angeles.*

Annika Fehling

Annika is a performing and recording Swedish singer-songwriter living in Visby, capital city of the magical island Gotland. With roots in Americana/folk/pop, Annika writes music for herself, other artists, theater, and art exhibitions. She tours in Germany, UK, Ireland, NL, USA, Greenland, Sweden, Norway, Denmark, Finland, and Estonia, with regular appearances on TV and radio, in Sweden and Europe.

Annika has 13 CD albums to her credit, the latest one with her trio A.F.T. called *In The Universe* (Rootsy/Warner, 2018) with musicians Christer Jonasson and Robert Wahlström. For more information, visit www.annikafehling.com or www. reverbnation.com/annikafehling.

Yvette Keller

Yvette lives in Santa Barbara, California, where she writes, produces audiobooks, and facilitates corporate training (whenever her dog isn't walking her on the beach). She is the author of *The Coven of The Bowler Stories*, published in *Enheduanna*, the Literary Journal of the Utah Pagan Society. She is the voice of Viola Roberts (and all the other characters too) for the Viola Roberts Cozy Mysteries.

Yvette is lucky enough to be pursuing her ultimate fantasy: Winning a Campbell, a Hugo, and celebrating at a fancy costume party with her literary heroes: Guy Gavriel Kay, Patricia McKillip, Mercedes Lackey, Mary Robinette Kowal, Stephen R. Donaldson, Neil Gaiman, and a cardboard cutout of Douglas Adams.

To learn more about Yvette visit www.yvettekeller.com, like her on FB at www.facebook.com/authoryvettekeller, or follow her on Twitter at @YvetteKeller.

M.K. Knight

M.K. is an IT professional with a love for science fiction, fantasy, and the supernatural. Born in Brooklyn and raised in Vermont, M.K. found her tribe and her home in Santa Barbara, California. She lives with her husband and a couple of cats.

Tom Layou

Tom lives in Alaska and has had journalistic work published in the *Anchorage Daily News*. Tom is a regular attendee of the Santa Barbara Writers Conference, where he won an award for best nonfiction at the age of eighteen. More recently he has been published in *Luna Review*. He pays his rent selling legal cannabis. Twitter: @tomlayou_writer, Instagram: tomlayou, Facebook: Tom Layou.

Gabrielle Louise

Gabrielle is a nationally touring troubadour noted for her poignant lyrics and lush voice. The daughter of two vagabond musicians, Gabrielle inherited the predisposition to wanderlust and song. Gabrielle Louise's music is anchored deeply in folk and Americana, but undeniably drawn to rich harmonies and melodic adventurism. Her sound has the earthy feel of early Joni Mitchell, while also veering into the spirited and versatile delivery of fellow genre-hopping artist Eva Cassidy. Unafraid to take a musical escapade in the name of inspiration, Gabrielle is at one moment folkie and ethereal, the next a smoky jazz chanteuse. You can visit her at www.gabriellelouise.com.

Shelly Lowenkopf

Emeritus from the graduate-level Professional Writing Program at USC, where he taught fiction, humor, and editing courses for thirty-four years, Shelly recently completed a visiting professorship at UCSB's College of Creative Studies.

He's held executive editorial positions with five different book publishers, including two in Santa Barbara. He's also put in time with literary, mystery, and science fiction magazines.

His latest book, *Love Will Make You Drink and Gamble, Stay Out Late at Night*, is a collection of recent short fiction. He's currently balancing a revised second edition of *The Fiction Writer's Handbook* with a collection of stories about the protagonist of the actor featured in this volume, and *Santa Barbara Sleep*, a mystery novel set in a local retirement complex.

Ian McCartor

Ian is a singer/songwriter, hospice nurse, and world traveler. He is originally from the high desert of Southern California, spending half the year working with his hospice patients and the other half traveling and writing new music. He also hosts international retreats in a castle located in the south of France, hosts the Song Soldier Podcast, and shows his artwork privately in galleries around the world. He shares his projects on IanMcCartor.com.

Jordan O'Halloran

Jordan lives in Cobb Mountain, California, with her boyfriend, roommate, and cat. She is a teen-family advocate at a nonprofit during the day, and any free time she has is spent writing. She won the Santa Barbara Writers Conference Best Fiction award in 2018. She is a big fan of bright colors, trees, the ocean, and soft cheese. She is grateful you took the time to read her story and hopes you enjoyed it. You can see more of her on Instagram and Facebook as Jordanjotsjoy.

Nate Streeper

Nate is a writer, runner, and gamer who spent his first eighteen years in Visalia and his latter twenty-five in Santa Barbara. His science fiction adventure novel, *Murder on the Orion Express*, was published in 2017. Streeper received an Honorable Mention for Humor from the Santa Barbara Writers Conference in 2018. His short stories and essays can be found on his website, natestreeper.com, whereas Streeper himself can be found running along the waterfront on most sunny afternoons.

Max Talley

Max is a writer and artist who was born in New York City and now resides in Southern California. Talley's fiction and essays have appeared in *Del Sol Review, Fiction Southeast, Gravel, Hofstra University—Windmill, Bridge Eight, Litro Magazine,* and *The Opiate,* among others. His near future novel, *Yesterday We Forget Tomorrow,* was published in 2014, and he teaches a writing workshop at the Santa Barbara Writers Conference. More art and writings at www.maxdevoetalley.com.

Terry Wolverton

Terry is the author of eleven books of poetry, fiction ,and creative nonfiction, including *Embers,* a novel in poems, and *Insurgent Muse: life and art at the Woman's Building,* a memoir. Her most recently collection of poetry is *RUIN PORN.* She is the founder of Writers At Work, a creative writing studio in Los Angeles, and Affiliate Faculty in the MFA Writing Program at Antioch University Los Angeles.

Chris Wozney

Chris has a degree in Liberal Arts from St. John's College and a master's from Chapman University. She spent four years as an Army medic, after which she became a teacher. She is married to a fellow former medic (they grok each other), and they have two wonderful children. Editing is her third career; she is the Senior Editor for Penmore Press in Tucson, AZ. Chris writes book reviews, primarily of fantasy and speculative fiction, to share her love of literature.

Robin Winter

Robin first wrote and illustrated a manuscript on 'Chickens and their Diseases' in second grade. Born in Nebraska, she's lived in a variety of places, Nigeria, New Hampshire, upper New York state, and California. She pursues a career in oil painting under the name of Robin Gowen, specializing in landscape, and her work can be viewed at Sullivan Goss Gallery in Santa Barbara. Robin is married to a paleobotanist, who corrects the science in both her paintings and her stories. She's published a handful of science fiction short stories. Her first novel, a historical thriller, *Night Must Wait,* came out through Imajin Books in 2012, her second, *Future Past* was published by Caliburn Press, and White Whisker Press published her third, *Watch the Shadows.*

Stephen T. Vessels

Stephen is a Thriller Award nominated author of science fiction, dark fantasy, and cross-genre ficiton. His stories have appeared in *Ellery Queen Mystery Magazine*, and collections from Grey Matter Press and ShadowSpinners Press. His story collection, *The Mountain & The Vortex and Other Tales* was released by Muse Harbor Publishing. He has written art and music reviews for the *Santa Barbara Independent* and is a published poet and visual artist. You can visit him at www.stephentvessels.com.

EDITORS

Silver Webb, Editrix

Silver conceived of the idea for the *Santa Barbara Literary Journal* while attending the Santa Barbara Writer's Conference in 2017. Listening to so many talented writers talk about the difficulty of finding places to publish, she thought, *I could do that.* Perhaps a foolish impulse. But Silver is, in fact, a professional editor who has designed publications before. She is a writer first, naturally, and her topic of choice for nonfiction is food (she writes for *Food & Home*), and for fiction, well, witches are a weakness. Witches who can cook are a double weakness. You can see more about Silver's writing and adventures at www.silverwebb.com or @bakery_babe.

Laura Hemenway, Mistress of Song

Laura curates our section of Lyrics, which endeavors to treat song lyrics with the same importance and eye as poetry.

Laura graduated from UCSB in 1976 with a master's degree in instrumental conducting. After a sucessful music career in Antelope Valley, she "retired" in 2009, and moved back to Santa Barbara with her husband, songwriter Dennis Russell. She plays cello with the SBCC Orchestra, sings in the women's vocal ensemble "Lux," and is a "regular" at Palm Loft Songwriter's Circle in Carpinteria. Laura has served as Music Director for Out of the Box Theatre, has played cello with the Santa Barbara Folk Orchestra, and has served on the board for the Goleta Valley Art Association.

Ron Alexander, Poetry Baron

Ron is a psychologist, long-term AIDS survivor, and poet. Much of his work reflects the absurdity he finds in living decades past his "Use-by" date. His work has appeared in journals including *Arts & Understanding, Askew, Solo Novo,* and *Lummox3,* as well as several anthologies, such as *A Bird Black as the Sun: California Poets on Crows & Ravens,* and *To Give Life a Shape.* One of four poems in a recent anthology, *Poems 2 F*ck 2,* "Zebra" inspired a short film of the same name by Paul Detwiler, which has been shown at LGBTQ film festivals in North and South America, Europe, and Asia.

Sharon Venezio, Guest Editor of Poetry

Sharon Venezio is the author of *The Silence of Doorways* (March 2013, Moon Tide Press). Her poems have appeared in numerous journals, including *Spillway, Bellevue Literary Review, Reed,* and elsewhere. She is also featured in the anthology *Wide Awake: Poets of Los Angeles and Beyond* as well as the anthology *Stone, River, Sky: an Anthology of Georgia Poems*. She lives in Ventura where she is also a behavior analyst specializing in autism. Read more at sharonvenezio.com.

95633317R00139

Made in the USA
San Bernardino, CA
16 November 2018